The Art of Motherung
of
Our Lives in Colour and Shadow

Karen D. Miller

Big Sister, Little Brother, 14" x 11", wool yarns and acrylic yarns on linen.
Karen D. Miller, Ottawa, Ontario, Canada, 2015.

Presented by

RUG HOOKING

Ampry Publishing, Northbrook, Illinois

Front Cover:
Motherhood Still Life #2: The Living Room, 38.5" x 30.5", wool yarns and acrylic yarns, acrylic paint on linen. Karen D. Miller, Ottawa, Ontario, Canada, 2019.

Snow Buddy, 14" x 11", wool yarns and acrylic yarns on linen. Karen D. Miller, Ottawa, Ontario, Canada, 2015.

Copyright © 2022 by Ampry Publishing LLC
Published by
AMPRY PUBLISHING LLC
3400 Dundee Road, Suite 220
Northbrook, IL 60062
www.amprycp.com

www.rughookingmagazine.com
Graphic design by Matt Paulson

Printed in the United States of America
10 9 8 7 6 5 4 3 2 1

Rug photos and photos of handwork by the artists, unless otherwise noted
Cover photographs by the author
All other photography by the author

Other books by Karen D. Miller
Eyes Open to the World: Memories of Travel in Wool (2019)

Cataloging-in-Publication Data
Library of Congress Control Number: 2022947232

ISBN 978-1-945550-63-8

Acknowledgments

The Slide, 14" x 11", wool yarns and acrylic yarns on linen. Karen D. Miller, Ottawa, Ontario, Canada, 2016.

To Kadyn & Peyton: Being your mum is my greatest gift. So many memories made and moments shared that I will never forget, and I can't wait for all of those still to come. You are both my friends and my muses and I could not be prouder of you both. Love you forever and ever.

Thank you to my husband, Daniel, for being my editor and for reassuring me that I shouldn't be afraid to put in the hard stuff. I love you.

To my own mother: I think I understand more. I wish we had had more time.

I have been so fortunate to be surrounded by some incredible mothers who have made the journey so much better: Christie Buchan, Michelle Chiu, Sarah Fisher-Reid, Jennifer Gagne, Simmone Hollingsworth, Christine Ivory, Mikki Jackson, Jennifer Koussaya-Kent, Kristen McCormick, Jennifer Pagnotta, Cassandra Polyzou, Laurie Proulx, Jen Saxe, Stephanie Tanton, Leigh Tronsgard, and Tanya Wackley. Although we may all not see each other as much as we did when our children were younger, know that the playdates, trips to the park, wine nights, and conversations made me feel that I was never alone and made the tough days lighter.

Thank you to Debra Smith, Mark Allison, and and Ampry Publishing for taking the leap to support the making of this book. And a tremendous thank you to all of the artists who contributed their amazing art to this book and who trusted me with their stories. I am forever grateful that you came along on this ride with me.

A Note on Motherhood

All of the artists in this book are cis-gendered women who had, tried to have, or contemplated having children. Of course, there are other perspectives on mothering and many other family arrangements. This book acknowledges but does not attempt to capture all of these perspectives. It exclusively portrays the perspectives of the 22 artists (including myself) who contributed to it.

Contents

Ripple Effect, 29.5" x 25", wool yarns and acrylic yarns on rug
warp. Karen D. Miller, Ottawa, Ontario, Canada, 2021.

In the Beginning

And now it begins. Except that of course this isn't where it began, because obviously this moment has always been a possibility for you. You thought about it. Maybe this has been your dream since you were still a child, and this is the first moment of your dream come true. Maybe this is something you've unexpectedly found yourself in, and you are equally terrified and excited for what it might turn out to be. Or maybe this is something you just felt that you had to do.

For me, motherhood has been the most demanding experience of my life. I know that it will be all-consuming if I let it, and so I struggle every day to make sure that I leave space for myself. As my kids are a little older now, I have had more time to look in the mirror and wonder about the choices I have made, where I am now, and what is to come. I haven't found any easy or completely satisfying answers. In fact, there are almost always perplexing contradictions and maddening loose ends that thwart my quest for clear rationalizations. How can anyone be both happy and disquieted by the same thing, at the same time? Because motherhood is complex, and so am I. And the two together? That's impenetrable. Which makes art the perfect vehicle for exploring it.

Art embraces these problems of duality and ambiguity. I can use it to poke at the uncomfortable questions in my life, and sometimes even make subtle little confessions to myself. And art, perhaps even more than motherhood, is a community where someone, somewhere, is always wrestling with the same questions that are troubling you. In art, just as in motherhood, there is absolutely no reason to be alone. That is where and how this book was born and grew to be the volume in your hands now, encompassing the collected views of 22 artists, including me. If you are a new mother beginning the journey that we began however many years ago, we want you to know that you aren't alone, and that what you are about to experience is as wonderful as everybody has been telling you—and as hard as they aren't really mentioning. Your feelings about all of this will be as unpredictable as the patterns in your child's kaleidoscope, and all of that is absolutely normal. We want you to be aware, because to be aware is to be empowered. If you are reading this book and you are already a mother, perhaps you will see a little bit of yourself and your own journey in some of these stories too.

But right here and right now, you have no time for any of this, for anyone or anything else, or even for you. You have just given birth, maybe for the first time, maybe for the fifth. It doesn't matter. Baby needs fed, there is a book full of firsts to come, and this whole little world is looking to you to make it all happen. Now.

Motherhood Still Life #4: Please Help, 19.5" x 16", wool and acrylic yarn on rug warp.
Karen D. Miller, Ottawa, Ontario, Canada, 2022.

1

The Paths to Here

Choice. It's not the first word that comes to mind when most people think about motherhood. If anything, motherhood is most often and infamously associated with our lack of choice over even the most basic aspects of our lives, like when to sleep and when to be at school pickups. But as I'll show throughout this book, choice is as central to motherhood as it is in any other aspect of our lives, just maybe trickier and more ephemeral. You will lose it, you will regain it, and you will have more degrees of it in some instances than in others. Some choices—and their consequences—will be plain while others will be more difficult to find. How you got here is only the first such choice in a lifetime of motherhood.

What especially fascinates me about this first choice, the choice to even be a mother, is that it begins to affect you long before you actually make it. More than likely, your family and friends have asked you when the "little ones" will start coming, and you've either played along with their innocent curiosity, or not. It is so much more than that, though, isn't it? People with influence over your life have made decisions that have affected your trajectory, sometimes openly, and oftentimes not. Prospective romantic partners have asked and heard your answer, and then drawn their own conclusions about your intentions. Some of us have attended job interviews knowing that the recruiter was transparently wondering only two questions: Will she? And when? And they definitely drew their own conclusions.

Many of us, myself included, have even been advised to have our children now instead of pursuing this or that job, or had solid leads dissolve into vague promises immediately after it was learned that we were pregnant. Those opportunities that I didn't get were pretty clear, but I'll never know about how many others I never even knew about. I'll never know what job prospects I wasn't told about, or which people I wasn't introduced to, or which people I was introduced to instead of others, all because people filled in their own answers to those two questions. All of the children that you might have? Yes, they have always been there with you.

Did I ever think about having or wanting children? Honestly no. I didn't think that they would fit with the plan that I had for my life. Now that they are here, though, I can't imagine my life without them. Because ultimately, like many women, I did make the choice. In my case, that decision was carefully taken, shaped by the best assumptions I could make about my life, my career, my partner, and the promises I was given about the future. Looking back, very little actually turned out either the way that I expected or that I was earnestly reassured it would. Evidently, life is complicated and not much given to heeding even the most fervent wishes.

There is one more important thing about the choice to be a mother that makes it truly unique in all the choices that any person can make. Many couples do go to the altar and vow until death do them part, but a quick check shows that the probability today of a change of heart on that commitment is about two in five. By comparison, even with custody arrangements, adoption, and foster care, the likelihood that your decision to be a mother will in fact be for life is much, much higher. It is unsurprising, then, that the decision to have children and the timing of their arrival are not choices that many women take lightly.

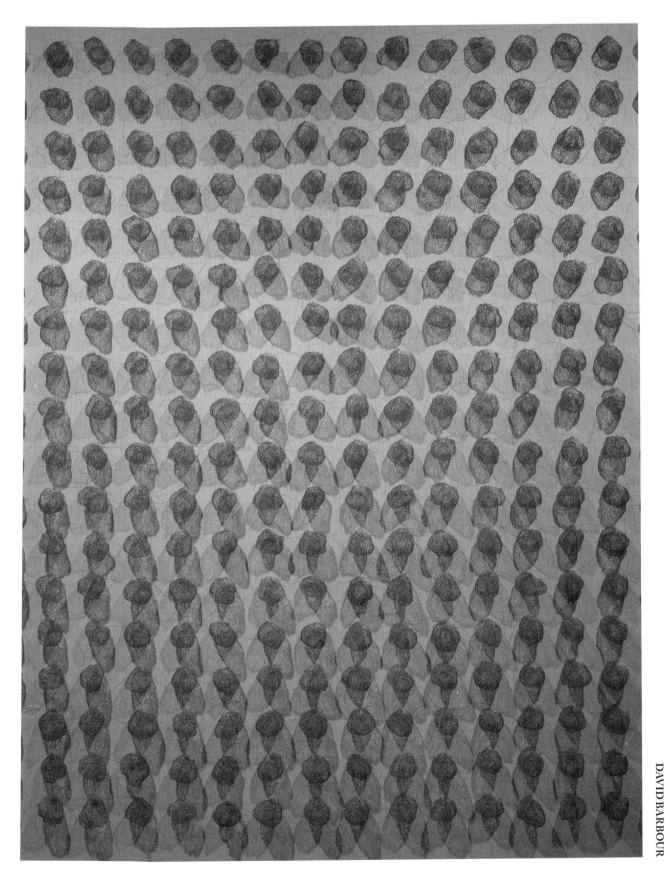

Ova, 79" x 79", hand-knitted copper wire. Sayward Johnson, Chelsea, Quebec, Canada, 2016–19.

Ova (detail).

Which is Sayward Johnson's purpose with *Ova* (previous page). The magic of Sayward's piece is that she isn't telling you what to think about fertility. Instead, what she is doing is presenting to you in one glance the scale of a woman's reproductive choice. Each of the 400 small orbs represents one of the 350 to 400 ova that, if you are an average woman, you will expect to release over your lifetime. In person, the installation takes up most of a good-sized wall, even reaching well above your head.

This collective, in its own right, is impressive enough in its expansive perspective of fertility. And yet, Sayward also draws you into the specifics of the choice you face every month. Every orb is hand knit out of copper wire; every single one is different. Obviously, each ovum has the potential to be fertilized, and so each orb represents the possibility of a different person. But it is also true that every ovum—if fertilized—represents a different pathway for your own life. So *Ova* invites you to plot out as well the life of the woman carrying these ova, her growth into adulthood, her career, and her partnerships.

And so there it is, the entire spectrum of fertility choices of a woman, for just over 30 years of her life from her mid-teens to her late forties. Through this time, she is continually balancing the future possibilities of all of these ova with living her own life. This dual complexity invites you to lose yourself in contemplation. What you make of it all, though, Sayward leaves to you, precisely because this choice is so deeply personal to every woman and because, of course, the unnamed, unknown woman on the wall is you. Where you are in your life, what your dreams are, and what hand fate has dealt to you will all define how you react to this piece.

Perhaps in *Ova* you see endless, indistinguishable cycles that you are managing because you want children, but not yet, or not again just now. Or perhaps you are drawn to find where you are now in life, to study which ovum is next to come because you are trying to conceive; each ovum in your past is an opportunity lost, and each one still to come is another chance. Perhaps you can point out which ones are the lives who are now standing beside you, those you wanted and brought into the world—and maybe even that you didn't particularly want but that came anyway. Maybe you quietly count out to those ova that tried and failed. Whatever your perspective, everyone shares the truth that after the last ovum, there is nothing more.

As it so happens, *Ova* is a deeply personal piece for Sayward. Creating it was one way for her to come to terms with the impending end of her own fertility, unfortunately compounded by life circumstances that did not support her and her partner having another child. That she was able to transform this specific experience into such a universal and inclusive portrayal of the multiple realities of fertility is a testament to her strength as an artist.

The rest of this book is, in a way, all about filling in some of the possibilities of *Ova* with the details of lives lived by 22 artists. With our art and the stories that we will share, we all wrestled in our own ways with the questions of when, how many, and many variants of the question "and now how am I supposed to—?"

We had many different perspectives on fertility. These differences have profound implications for how we see ourselves, but also our perceptions of other women and society at large. Some of us in this book knew that we wanted children of our own from a young age and so, happily, it came to pass. Others of us were just as categorical that in our youth we were resolute and emphatic that we did not want children at all. We had lots of reasons for not wanting children, or at least for hesitating about the decision. For example, many of us were clear eyed about who was going to bear the majority of the physical and emotional burden of raising the kids. Others shared their perspective that childhood is hard on children, too, and that they wanted to spare prospective children all the inevitable difficulties they would have to face in growing up.

But life happens, and in this as in all other things, situations and thinking changes. For some of us, this change in views was gradual, perhaps even imperceptibly so over a long time until the day came that we decided to do exactly that which we had once so categorically rejected. No discussion of fertility can avoid the famous biological clock, and some of us did experience it as an "intense biological and emotional desire" to have our own children. For others, we wished to avoid the regret that we feared would follow if we decided against having children. And, unfortunately, some of us had difficulties with conceiving and were forced to really evaluate why we wanted children before undertaking all the effort and expense that comes with fertility treatments and other medical interventions.

Balancing all of these considerations and taking the time to understand ourselves and our own complicated feelings about this important choice would be difficult enough if it were just ourselves that we had to worry about. But, although I wish I could say otherwise, we all know that it isn't that simple, and that parenting is just one of those topics upon which everyone around us thinks they are an expert. I confess that I was well aware of these pressures myself, and I thought I knew very well what opinions would come up, but I was still surprised by the breadth and impact of all of the stories that these women shared with me.

In my own experience, the idea that anyone can balance education, career, and children is just laughable; it is really a question of controlled sacrifice. As I recounted earlier, others who controlled my opportunities felt free to effectively make my decisions for me. What I hadn't realized was how lucky I was. Some of us, I learned, were even terminated from jobs after revealing a pregnancy. Many of us had our careers affected to different degrees,

though never positively. When taken in combination with the cost of raising a child, choosing to become a mother can even leave us uniquely vulnerable to control by our partners.

Neither is just focusing on being a mother any refuge. Our choice to have only one child is subject to debate, and likewise our choice in having what others consider too many children. And if we should terminate a pregnancy? This, unfortunately, is still a polarizing choice about which very few out there do not have strongly voiced opinions. Reading these honest accounts both sobered and saddened me. We all hope that we outgrow peer pressure when we leave school and that centuries of progress have taken us beyond "barefoot and pregnant," but it is clear that for women, strong vestiges of both remain.

And what if you should choose not to have children at all? I know that you already know the answer to that. You have almost certainly heard the views about your principal value to society being as a mother, and all about the nobility of the "greatest act of creation." I heard all of that, too, but in my case, I was able to brush it off because obviously it largely went away when I chose to have children. But for all that there may have been good, supportive intentions behind those words, two things bothered me about them. The first was that for the years that I was living my life without children, those words left no space for me. What value did I have, not being a mother? I know the answer because I do know women who chose not to have children. I know how they were labelled as career focused, and how that same term, while a high compliment for a man, was certainly not intended kindly for them. Not far behind, sometimes spoken but often hinted, was the aspersion that they don't like children and were therefore somehow unnatural for denying their biological destiny.

The second thing that bothered me was who was saying these things: often older men looking at me through the lens of their own values and assumptions while they pigeonholed my potential. That, I found harder to take. While I got over it and am living my life, I have never subscribed to the theory that I should just let those things lie. I prefer to think that we are capable of building a world where every young girl out there will be free to just get on with living her own life.

Yet another problem with such unnecessary and unhelpful words is that they offer no place in the world for the woman who can't have children. The truth is quite different. *Couldn't* is Linda Rae Coughlin's depiction of the reality of infertility and childlessness. She was "crushed but not surprised" when she learned that she and her husband would never have children of their own. However, in her telling, just as every woman's approach to motherhood is the product of her own choices, so too must every woman's approach to life without children be her own choice. In Linda Rae's case, she hadn't thought about having children all her life and had already spent much of her teenage years caring for her siblings. So, while the doctor's words were difficult to hear, they weren't the end of a lifelong dream. She is clear that the hurt was deep, but she found the path to move forward.

She and her husband did explore other possibilities for having children, but when those failed, she was able to embrace her life "not as a curse, but as a different type of blessing."

> For women around the world, pregnancy and child-rearing can interrupt education, isolate women, or make them vulnerable to patriarchal control.
>
> Nadine Flagel

> I assume I would've been far more industrious—maybe even great at something—had we not had children, but I also know I would have regretted it. That would have been an unfillable empty space.
>
> Amy Meissner

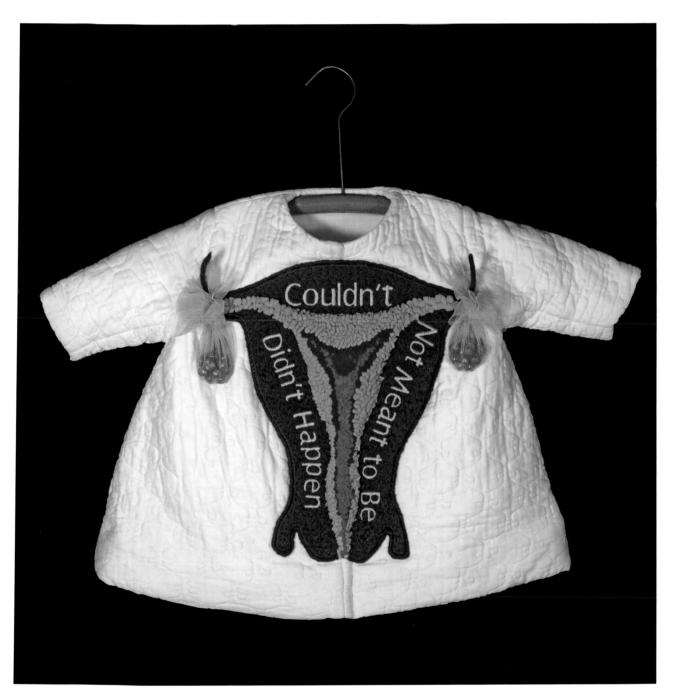

Couldn't, 21" x 24" x .5", hand-dyed recycled nylon, cotton, tulle, felt, and beads on linen and mounted on an antique quilted baby jacket. Linda Rae Coughlin, Warren, New Jersey, USA, 2019.

2

Help Wanted: Supermom

Now that you're in it, you will have quickly realized that you have been hired into one of the hardest jobs in the world. Your new boss is completely unreasonable, unable to clearly communicate even the simplest of requests, prone to imposing the most ludicrous demands on a whim, and possessing a supernova of a temper that requires no apparent cause for ignition. Your working conditions, if they can even be described as such, would violate every known workplace regulation. In fairness, you do have regular hours—those being 24/7—so you know better than to try to plan anything else in your life.

And your coworkers? Well, they might be around, or they might not, but they are certainly content in the knowledge that you have everything covered. When they randomly choose to helicopter in and lend a hand, they expect you to be grateful and to smile beatifically as they collect all of the plaudits for their demonstration of selfless dedication and commitment. The entire job description is unclear, as there never was any advertisement. One thing that is certain, though, is that it is impossible to tell exactly what, if anything, you aren't responsible for. It certainly includes everything that you were doing before, because this isn't just a new job. No, this is an extra job. And as for the pay, well, don't worry about that.

What kind of woman would sign up for this job?

Alexandrya Eaton has the obvious answer: supermom. In *Supermoms*, she uses an anonymous female figure

sporting a cape to represent the "woman being," which can be taken to mean either a community of women, or an individual travelling through her own "arsenal of superpowers." Being a mother is what has defined Alexandrya the most, but she admits that at times she feels that it requires the "superhuman powers" of a superwoman or a supermom to keep up with all of the expectations and requirements of the role.

Alexandrya has been a working artist all through her time as a mother. She tried to "have it all," as some people out there keep insisting is possible, trying to keep up the work schedule that she had had before having children. After years of multitasking—and I'm guessing superhuman amounts of patience and stamina—she realized not only that she was trying to achieve the unattainable, but that she didn't have to. She wasn't trying to meet anybody else's expectations, but rather her own—and they were unrealistic. Once she accepted that the only person she had to please was herself, she gained a sense of freedom, and control over her own life. She adjusted her own expectations of what she could accomplish with kids. She was able to shift her work schedule to accommodate her daughters' needs and to sever working relationships that were not supportive of her being both an artist and a mother.

> I can't do it all, I can't have it all, and I don't want it all, but I do want sustainability for myself, my emotions, and my family landscape.
>
> **Amy Meissner**

> For better or for worse, motherhood is about carrying the weight of others—both physically and emotionally.
>
> **Emily van Lidth de Jeude**

Supermoms, 30" x 60", wool on burlap. Alexandrya Eaton, Sackville, New Brunswick, Canada, 2020.

Michele Micarelli's *My Family Circus* draws the parallel between a circus and a household to represent the multiple roles that mothers take on to raise a family. The comparison is apt because while both are "mostly fun," there can be no mistaking the amount of unseen, background work that goes on to give the outward appearance of a "well-oiled machine," or how it is "an enormous challenge" for one person. Michele depicts herself as the clown whose job is to "keep everyone happy," a refrain that will be familiar to mothers everywhere.

Michelle has the added perspective of now watching her daughter and daughter-in-law raising their own children, and how they are having to keep everything in balance and "not letting any of the balls drop." They have become the tightrope walker and the juggler, respectively, two more motifs that every mother in the world will not just recognize, but feel, instantly.

> I do find holidays tricky. There's so much organization, and I find that after I get all the food, toys, sports equipment, tickets, clothes, etc. organized for everyone else, I don't even have the energy to get dressed and feed myself, let alone get my stuff all together and drive or fly somewhere. And have fun.
>
> Nadine Flagel

Marks of Motherhood II, 5" x 5", rust-dyed wool yarn on linen. Karen D. Miller, Ottawa, Ontario, Canada, 2018.

My Family Circus, 43" x 30", hand-dyed wool, yarn, silk, charms, beads, ribbon, and seashells on linen.
Michele Micarelli, New Haven, Connecticut, USA, 2020.

For Carmen Bohn, the biggest struggles she has faced since becoming a mother have been the lack of time to complete tasks and the almost constant feeling of being scattered as the "unrelenting hyperactivity" of motherhood leaves her, like so many, trying to find balance between all of the different roles that she plays.

Her piece *This Is the Unfinished Story of So Many Things No. 2* took her over 100 hours to weave, and she says that time was often interrupted. She says that "she never sat down for a good day or even a few good hours to make the piece" as she was always being asked for something, by someone. For Carmen, that is the story of the piece: the unfinished nature of so many things that we do as mothers. Her colour and material choices were chosen specifically to represent the contradictory feelings of motherhood: continuity and chaos, calm and over-whelmed, and playfulness with just a little bit of seriousness.

Yet there is a strip of orange woven through the piece which suggests a "ray of sunshine." There is a "silver lining" in the puffy blue and white roving, perhaps hinting that as her daughters grow, she will be able to carve out more and more time for herself to create. Carmen has left loose ends hanging off the right-hand side of the piece to signify "continuation" and the idea that because of competing demands on her time and attention everything is in an "unfinished state." The piece "undulates" when hung on the wall, both for aesthetic reasons and also mimicking "the ebb and flow of life" as the seasons of motherhood change.

Marks of Motherhood III, 6" round, rust-dyed wool yarns on linen. Karen D. Miller, Ottawa, Ontario, Canada, 2021.

This is the Unfinished Story of So Many Things No. 2, 38" x 33", hand-spun yarns, fabric, yarn, recycled sari silk, t-shirt, and mirror. Carmen Bohn, Ottawa, Ontario, Canada, 2021.

This Is the Unfinished Story of So Many Things No. 2 (detail).

down at my bowl of fruit—my oh-so-glamorous Old Masters still life moment. It perfectly encapsulated for me the duality of motherhood. At the same time that I was amused by his carefree presence that so enriches my own perspective on life every day, I was also thinking "great, one more pile of other people's stuff that I have to pick up and put away." Taking care of others almost all of the time is physically and mentally demanding, and while I want to be appreciative of every moment, like all of the older mothers are always telling me that I should, it is impossible to do so.

> I discovered that motherhood is a dance of bowing low down and leaping up high. It's a tug of war and love between giving away and running away. It's a dance with our children and our partners, and with ourselves.
>
> **Emily van Lidth de Jeude**

I explore some of my own feelings about the life that I lead now as a mother in my *Motherhood Still Life* series. Perhaps I am being a bit intemperate by gently mocking the Old Masters, but really, how much more plainly could they have paraded their male perspective? I don't think there is anywhere outside of the moneyed patriarchy where life could ever be so quiet that a bowl of fruit can be ornamental, that a vase of flowers can sit unmolested in a sunbeam, or especially that naked young women will pose for you day after day. As much as I studied their technique, I couldn't help but critique their compositions. Still lifes? My life is full of still life compositions; I probably pick up dozens every day. I decided that it would be healthy for the world to see life from a rather different perspective, the perspective of a contemporary mother.

The idea for *Motherhood Still Life #1: After the Bath* came to me while studying the works of the late Canadian painter Mary Pratt. I was really taken with the way she turned everyday items, and overall domesticity in general, into subjects for her work. So I was primed when my young son dumped all of his bath toys into the bathtub, played happily with them, and then got out, dried himself with a towel that he then, of course, threw on the floor, and walked away to do other things. As the water drained from the tub, I realized that I was looking

Motherhood Still Life #1: After the Bath, 25" x 20", wool and acrylic yarns on linen.
Karen D. Miller, Ottawa, Ontario, Canada, 2019. Frame by Daniel MacDonald.

Motherhood Still Life #2: The Living Room, 38.5" x 30.5", wool and acrylic yarns and acrylic paint on linen.
Karen D. Miller, Ottawa, Ontario, Canada, 2019. Frame by Daniel MacDonald.

I grew up, as I am sure many of you did, with the now-quaint notion that the living room was the one room in the house where kids should not play, and definitely should not leave their toys. The better furniture filled this space, while the television and toys and games were consigned to the more lived-in-looking family room, or the basement, or anywhere else out of sight and not underfoot. When guests arrived, they would be ushered quickly and directly into the living room, the one pristine, adult-oriented space always kept meticulously preserved as though it was a museum to another improbable time.

Of course, it was my mother's responsibility to keep this space immaculate at all times, on perpetual stand-by for the guests who came—let's be honest—once in a while at best. It was my mother's responsibility to keep the rest of the house tidy and organized, too, though the purpose of this was less clear to me even then. It was just that way, with my own mother and my friends' mothers, too: the house had to be clean enough to withstand surprise inspection. I remember it well, not so much for how clean all of the houses always were, even when I was invited in unexpectedly by a friend, but for how jarring it was whenever I came across an unexpected slip in the mask of perfection. A bath towel showing signs of having been recently used? A hand towel less than perfectly fluffy? A door left ajar to an untidy bedroom? The standard is still real, nowadays usually called having pride in your appearance or your place, or some such nonsense. It is quite impervious to how many children you have, or whether you were busy all day caring for them at home, or were busy all day away at work, or even whether or not having a tidy and clean house is a priority for you at all.

Motherhood Still Life #2: The Living Room is a scene from my own living room, from one of those rare days when I had fresh-cut flowers to show. We brought out a glass bowl for the occasion—a bowl that we acquired before we had kids, when a glass bowl still seemed a sensible souvenir to buy. We even put in some fruit that hadn't gone mushy yet. My living room, you see, is not my mother's living room. It is as lived in as any other part of my house. A bin of Lego lives semipermanently beside one chair—and Lego is a famously migratory toy that quickly populates every nook of any room it inhabits. So if you pop in to see me unexpectedly, you can expect to have to watch your step. There is no perfection on display because I am not perfect, and I don't expect anybody else to be perfect either.

> We are all imperfectly perfect. That is what makes us complete, don't you think?
>
> Rachelle Leblanc

Motherhood Still Life #3: Nude Study is a scene that confronted me—and there is truly no better word than that for the situation—one day when I went into the bathroom. That is just one of the realities of motherhood: that you are only ever imperfectly in control and life is full of surprises, both innocent and contrived, and both good and bad. On this occasion, my eldest child had gathered up all of the dolls in the house, removed all of their clothes in preparation for washing them, and then dumped them unceremoniously on the bathroom counter before going off to cause trouble somewhere else. The unintentional effect, well, that is what you wish to make of it. But even if rather more risqué than the conventional compositions, it was still as close as I am ever going to get in my life to having a model, or rather models, sit for me.

Marks of Motherhood IV, 10" x 10", rust-dyed wool yarn on linen and mounted on metal screen and a cotton scarf. Karen D. Miller, Ottawa, Ontario, Canada, 2017.

Motherhood Still Life #3: Nude Study, 26.5" x 38", wool and acrylic yarns on linen.
Karen D. Miller, Ottawa, Ontario, Canada, 2020. Frame by Daniel MacDonald.

Rachelle Leblanc carries all of these themes a step further in *Hands Full*, a depiction of a young mother standing on a hope chest and struggling to balance her children in her arms. The mother's balance is precarious as she attempts to wrap her arms around her children, but her reach falls tenuously short—not falling critically short, but neither providing the security of a more certain grasp. In this way, Rachelle conveys that motherhood is often full of "multitasking, anxiety, and worry" even at the same time as mothers are providing their children with "unconditional love."

In setting out this challenge, Rachelle is able to draw out the consequences of this balancing act on a mother's self-confidence. The whole job of mothering is made more difficult when women have "self-perceived short-comings." Rachelle herself "struggled with mom guilt," which meant that she often felt afraid that she was "not enough for her children," or was "unable to be who they needed her to be at all times." Rachelle also points out that this is not something reserved for mothers of young children, either, but that it continues on even when our children are grown.

This observation about the effect of our own self-perception on our ability to mother hints at another important reality: that the role of mother can even—and often does—change who we are. We will explore these changes in our self-identity in the next chapter.

> I haven't mothered anyone before, so I often don't feel like I know what I am doing.
>
> April DeConick

> I found it difficult to manage the housework. I often compared myself to other mothers who I thought had it all together—clean houses, tidy kids, great wardrobes.
>
> Meryl Cook

Hands Full, 41" x 17" x 8", cashmere, wool on linen, cotton thread, linen, polyester fill, wood, earthenware, medium fire glaze.
Rachelle Leblanc, Katy, Texas, USA, 2015.

3

Our Changing Self

It is impossible to be fully aware of the challenges of motherhood before it happens, no matter how much you might think that you know or how much you think that you are prepared for it. When I learned that I was pregnant with my first child, I knew my life was going to change, and it scared me. My husband promised me emphatically that nothing would change, and that we would keep living just the way that we had been. How little he knew. And, in hindsight, how little I knew. I just had no concept of how becoming a mother is the most complete and permanent change of a woman's life. I was young enough that I was still entirely preoccupied with learning who I was and who I could be, but that all ended when the baby arrived. I turned definitively from myself. I became instead the provider of another person's life.

> **Kids crack open your life and all kinds of crazy stuff comes out and flows in.**
>
> **Nadine Flagel**

Any other life change of this scale probably comes with counselling, training, or licensing. Yet when we enter into motherhood, there is a presumption that every woman has the innate ability and desire to be a mother, and that—conveniently enough for everybody else concerned—everything will be just fine with a little time.

Of course, this isn't true, or at least isn't nearly so neat and tidy. Even when we are happy and embracing our motherhood role, we can't forget that we are more than mothers, too. Like any adults, we have our own thoughts, curiosity, and feelings, and we know that every meaningful story in life has two sides, and often more. There is nothing in any of that that compromises our qualities as mothers or that we have to feel guilty about. Yet many artists I approached declined to participate in this project when I asked about the adversity and difficulties that they

faced as mothers. They assured me that everything had always been wonderful. This reaction was so common, in fact, that I became used to it, and even anticipated it. I knew I wasn't wrong to feel the way that I do, but it bothered me that so many women were being so unfair to themselves. Denying the challenges that they faced only trivializes the effort that they put in and the sacrifices that they made to launch their new beings into the world. Or maybe it really was always easy and wonderful for them, but I find that very unlikely.

> **Daughters become mothers, repeating, perhaps, an infinite cycle.**
>
> **Laura Salamy**

I do understand why they would not want to acknowledge the hard parts. Speaking about our difficult feelings can feel like a betrayal of our children; like you somehow compromise your love for them by acknowledging the difficulties that you had to prevail over. But at the same time, I can't help believing that it is a disservice to our children to shield them from the truth. One day it may be them or their partner who is the mother. Why perpetuate a myth? It is far better, in my opinion, to be truthful and to trust in the maturity of our children to understand that there are parts of mothering that are hard, and that it doesn't mean that we love them any less for it.

Speaking for myself, I am happy to be a mother. But sitting here on a sunny spring day some 14 years after having begun this journey, it occurs to me just how complex that tag—mother—is as an identity. For one, it isn't even all mine to define. Just like the champions we see in sports whose success is defined by the rivals who pushed them to reach greatness, so too is my identity as a mother inextricably linked to the aptitudes and accomplishments of my children. The comparison to sports is also fascinating for being so different. An athlete's story is all about the struggle to reach the top. It is about the years of training, the pain, the surgeries and the injuries, the bad luck, the failures, and the dark times that are overcome before fame and fortune are awarded. Nothing worthwhile comes without sacrifice and dedication.

I don't need to tell you that it is different with motherhood, but I won't go into why that is here. I won't document the sacrifice and dedication that is required to make any mothering work, and I won't be making any relativistic arguments about who sacrifices more. Rather, what is more interesting to me is the effect that mothering has on our own characters. It had many effects on me—so many in fact that 14 years later there are times when I can scarcely recognize any longer who I once was. In their own myriad ways, and as I will share in this chapter, all of the artists in this book experienced the same thing. For better and for worse, motherhood is a transformative experience. Obviously that transformation varies in scale from person to person according to their personality and their circumstances, but it is an unavoidable part of the experience. And that, to me, is the great shame about burying the social realities of mothering under simple assumptions about the role of women. It also buries all of the fascinating details about what can be a complex turning point in a woman's life.

I can most easily show what I mean with the most obvious—and most clichéd—point: motherhood, most obviously in the early days, months, and years, is a selfless endeavour. I'm looking here at a definition that describes selflessness as a combination of attentiveness to the needs of others and lack of preoccupation with your own interests, advancement, and desires. I am challenged to think of another domain outside of motherhood where this definition truly applies.

> Everyone has seen me naked or breastfeeding—I have nothing left to hide.
>
> Nadine Flagel

Marks of Motherhood V, 3.5" x 3.5", rust-dyed yarn on linen, fabric. Karen D. Miller, Ottawa, Ontario, Canada, 2017.

Especially in those early days. Children need an endless stream of diaper changes, need to be fed (and what a nightmare that can be!) and burped so that they stop screaming, and they need to be held when they decide that they need holding, usually uncannily opposite to the cycle of the sun. If one has any ego at all, the early years of motherhood are a doctorate in humility. Others in this book described this experience as the unending physical and mental labour of motherhood, when we cease to be the star in our own movie and, very pointedly, when it's not about you anymore.

And as all mothers know, this never ends. The needs just change: making sure they don't fall and bump their heads as they learn to walk, putting up baby gates so they don't tumble down the stairs, constant vigilance to ensure they don't put small objects in their mouths and choke, or put metal objects in the electrical sockets, or any number of possibilities that you couldn't ever have imagined. Then come school dropoffs and pickups, extracurricular activities to get to, clothes to buy for growing bodies, haircuts and appointments to keep up with. And I am forewarned that I still have the thankless teenage years to look forward to, when I will be a necessary third wheel in the life of a budding adult who is navigating that awkward space between need and independence.

In my own experience, subjugating one's self isn't easy to do. In fact, I am very open that it is difficult, and I am proud of what I have been able to do. I am proud of the challenges that I faced and overcame, and I am proud of how it all came together. Likewise, I congratulate all those mothers who succeeded as well, because I understand. I understand that motherhood is in general a messy and imperfect process full of "rough edges and frayed seams," and things happen along the way that hurt, that we regret, that sting, and that scar us for life. This is the cost of our selflessness to our little beings, and I bear my marks proudly.

> One thing I had realized is that having children is not a task that you can finish. Children keep changing!
>
> **Nadine Flagel**

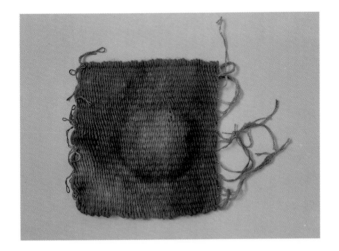

Marks of Motherhood VI, 6" x 5.5", rust-dyed wool yarns. Karen D. Miller, Ottawa, Ontario, Canada, 2018.

My *Marks of Motherhood* series that you see throughout this book is my homage to all the unavoidable dings and scratches—and worse—that I have accumulated so far in my motherhood journey, whether physical, mental, or emotional. Their imperfect and sometimes battered appearances are a nod to things that you can see, like my stretch marks, my c-section scars, and the dark circles that are usually under my eyes. They also represent things that you can't see, like my overcrowded and muddled brain, my aching back and shoulders, and the energy that I expend clinging to my aspirations for my future. I used natural and rust-dyeing techniques because—just like motherhood—it required that I give up perfect control of the results and give in to the process. The results, which are governed by the ways the dyes soak into the textiles, mimic the ways in which I was, and continue to be, transformed by being a mother.

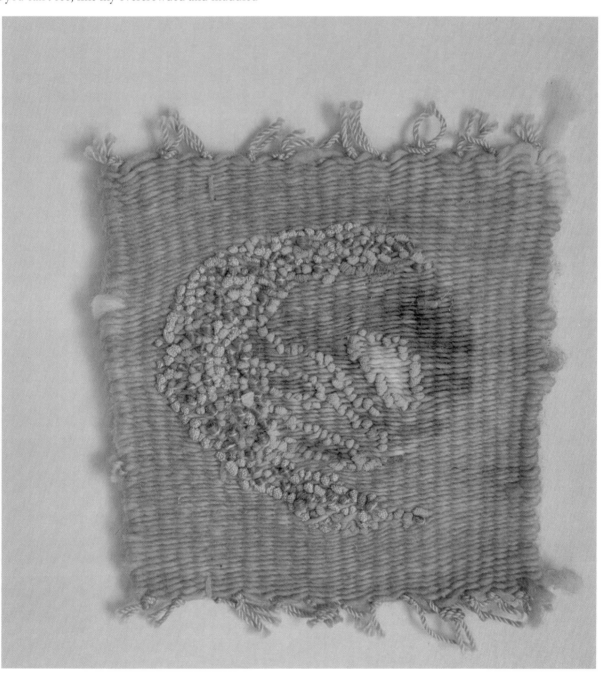

Marks of Motherhood VII, 5" x 5.5", rust-dyed wool yarns and nylon stockings.
Karen D. Miller, Ottawa, Ontario, Canada, 2018.

Holes documents the multiple changes that Laura Salamy experienced in motherhood. It is an explicitly autobiographical piece, bounded by the life-sized outline of her own body. The three holes that Laura has placed within her profile represent some of what she calls the "unpatchable and irreversible" holes that motherhood leaves behind. While the holes are directly symbolic of Laura's own experience, her art still reaches out to a wider audience because it evokes changes to which many mothers will relate. For example, the hole in the abdomen is unfortunately literal. It refers to the actual holes that scarred Laura's uterus after her miscarriages, before she had her daughter. Many women will relate to this because, although reported statistics vary, some 10 to 20 percent of known pregnancies will end in miscarriage.

The hole in the head represents multiple aspects of "brain drain." The first aspect refers to her pregnancy. I think most mothers remember this, and indeed how our forgetfulness and scattered concentration was expected, and maybe even an object of lighthearted fun for those around us. And why wouldn't it be? After all, pregnancy so distorts our form and robs us of any grace in our movements that forgetfulness probably seems a natural part of the pregnancy package.

As Laura notes, though, and as many women will relate, brain drain doesn't end with childbirth. Holes is also referring to the loss of ability to concentrate that she suffered later as she faced the testing challenge of raising a "difficult" child. This had an unfortunate consequence for Laura in that, as a writer, losing her ability to concentrate meant that she had to give up her love for writing fiction. While I have not had Laura's experience to that degree, I am familiar with the energy drain that comes from endlessly anticipating and meeting the needs of another being and the mind muddle that comes from multitasking so continuously that we become conditioned never to focus on anything. Trying to think in the same way that we used to do isn't impossible, but it certainly requires a lot more effort.

The hole that Laura placed over her heart evokes the duality of motherhood. Laura lost her heart to her daughter before she was even born. I understand that, and I think that probably every mother will attest to the same. But it also represents heartache, and the one doesn't come without the other. Loving another so completely means that we are absolutely invested in their lives. Whenever things don't turn out for them like we hope, we will feel the pain. If their childhood is difficult, we will feel more pain because loving less is not a choice. Laura shows this with little hearts all over her body. There is no accident in their placement. She has positioned them over her pulse points, to illustrate the unequivocal love she has for her daughter, no matter the pain.

> Ultimately, I am a vessel; life put holes in me. A bucket with holes is potentially useless. A watering can with its intentional holes is not.
>
> Laura Salamy

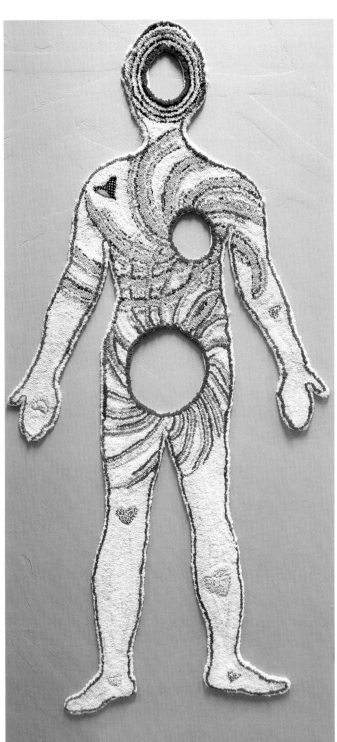

Holes, 68" x 33" x 0.75", recycled textiles, silk sari yarn, and cotton binding on monk's cloth. Laura Salamy, Albuquerque, New Mexico, USA, 2020.

GARY LAMOTT

Shadow Self, 66" x 66", abandoned embroideries, cotton, velvet, and linen.
Amy Meissner, Anchorage, Alaska, USA, 2019.

Think about *Ova* (p. 3) again for a moment, and all of those life possibilities on the wall. How different does that wall look to a woman who fervently wishes for children and to a woman who has no interest in children at all? And, more intriguingly, does that wall look the same to you after you take your decision? Amy Meissner explores the relationship between societal perception and self-identity in *Shadow Self*. In short, what if what you feel isn't what you are supposed to feel? What then?

She is referring to the presumption that every woman's goal, and indeed some would say her defining purpose, is motherhood. But what if you have your child, and you unquestionably love them, but you can't deny that you also feel something else, too? What if having invested yourself wholly in the endeavour that is motherhood, you realize that who you are now is different, and that you miss who you were before? Is that normal? Is it normal to wonder what your life would have been like if you hadn't had children?

Amy believes that all mothers do feel a change in their sense of self, and that many feel a sense of loss for the self that they once were. That was her experience, and many others in this book expressed similar thoughts. The problem, Amy believes, is that we aren't encouraged to be open about this, and so nobody acknowledges it. As a result, every woman is left to process these feelings herself, unaware that she is far from alone.

Further, Amy pondered, what of a woman who either can't or doesn't want to have children? Perhaps she might wonder the reverse, about what her life would have held for her had she had children. Even if not, Amy considered what it must be like to be on another path when so many of those around you are presuming that of course you must want motherhood. Where, she might wonder, is her place in the world, and why isn't it just as valid?

Amy wove together these two perspectives of Mother and of Other to create *Shadow Self*. Her work uses the reverse sides of abandoned embroideries to present motherhood as "all knots and loose ends, far from ideal and never meant to be seen." For Amy, honouring these reverse sides and making them central to her work is the "opportunity to reveal a gritty underbelly, an imperfect facet of motherhood, a false expectation society places on women." For those who are trying to process these complicated feelings, Amy's message is simple: "you aren't alone, your feelings are normal, and it's human to harbour, even hide, a shadow self."

An important part of your identity is bound up in your relationships, and motherhood changes those, too. But that isn't all that surprising. In the beginning, motherhood is such a limiting and all-consuming experience that only those who have shared the experience can really understand what you are going through behind the facade. Of course, you will gravitate towards those who understand you and who can empathize with what you are feeling. Mommy groups are real, and I was thankful for mine after having each of my children. They got me out of the house, I got to talk to other adults who used complete words and formed whole thoughts, and they often had tips that made life just that little bit easier. I thought it was amazing how motherhood brought together so many so very different people who had often travelled in completely different social circles before becoming mothers.

The intensity of motherhood has consequences for almost all of our other relationships. Many of us in this book found that it was difficult to keep friendships going with friends who didn't have children. Just as many mothers find a common bond through their shared intense experience, the opposite is often true for mothers and their friends without children. The mother finds not only that her time is at a premium, but that she also lacks the limitless reserves of patience to explain to everyone else why she is unavailable, or that she was available and now isn't, or that she just doesn't want to be available at all right now. I've been on the other side of it, too, when somebody I knew had a child before I was a mother myself. You try to be understanding but after a while it just becomes difficult to keep the friendship going.

And for those glamour couples who have a child to save a relationship? With the benefit of life lived, I can't imagine a more hopeless plan. The artists in this book found that parenting invariably magnified any perceived imbalances in household responsibilities within our relationships. The parenting responsibilities won't be equally shared, and the sacrifices won't be the same for each of you, because you'll always be given reasons why they can't. Watching your spouse or partner still doing many—if not all, or even more—of the things that they did before your children came can be very grating, no matter what you may have agreed beforehand about how life was going to go.

> I always wondered if I would want to be a stay-at-home parent. But it turns out, no—I'm a better mother when I'm a working mother.
>
> Nadine Flagel

Careers were the most common element of self-identity that the artists in this book raised with me. If, like in my case, a large part of your identity before having a child was tied to your career, then how you choose to mother becomes a particularly complicated decision. Making the choice between returning to work or staying at home to care for your children is not a straightforward one, and we all felt judged no matter which option we chose. Many had financial reasons for returning to the workforce or found that the cost of childcare was prohibitive, particularly after the second child. But many were also clear that the choice was not purely an economic one. Retaining our sense of self and continuing to do something that we love and find rewarding is also an important consideration in any mother's decision to return to her career. In fact, some found that working made them much better mothers and happier people.

For something so important to so many of us, it probably bears mentioning how these women reconciled a career with children. Full-time employment is, as the name suggests, full time, and there are obviously no breaks from parenting. Choices have to be made, and several women explained how they took a longer view and made their choice in the context of their lifetime rather than just the here and now. For many, this meant waiting to have children. This enabled them to devote their full energies to completing their education and successfully establishing themselves in their careers. Some did extensive travelling and other things that they knew they would be unable to do when they had less time. This preparation meant that when they decided to have children, the sacrifices they made were a pleasure and not a burdensome challenge because they weren't sacrificing the opportunity to live parts of their lives; they'd already done them. It made them less resentful of the inevitable changes in their career paths that came with motherhood.

Others tried more directly to balance staying in their career with having children, which is a more day-to-day undertaking. Choosing to work part-time while their children were young, for example, helped to keep their link to the workplace until they were ready to return to full-time work when their children reached school age. This approach required continuous juggling to make it work. They had to restrict the hours that they could take on, and they often had to take days off from work to be able to meet all of their children's needs.

And some women elected to stay at home, feeling that they just did not want to miss out on those early years of their child's development. They decided to stay at home with their children, even if in many cases it meant a financial sacrifice for the family. Others had the choice effectively made for them because their spouse moved so frequently that finding so many new and understanding employers was too challenging. There is no right answer, of course. Many of the women in this book, no matter what choice they made, told me of their bouts of self-doubt as to whether or not they had made the right one.

I am SAHM.

I am SAHM.

SAHM I am.

Do you like a star-shaped ham;

a toasted peanut-butter jam;

Mrs. Mama Mother Ma'am;

singing songs ad nauseam?

Rocking reading smocking feeding

Cooking thrice but never eating

Warm.

I am SAHM.

Again again again again!

Running away into the rain,

I would not could not read, my brain

has gone quite quickly quite insane.

And he comes home and says I've got

so much more time for stirring thought!

Not.

I am SAHM.

Excerpt from *Stay at Home Mom* by Emily van Lidth de Jeude

As for me, my choice was to stay at home. It wasn't something I'd dreamed about—quite the opposite in fact. I always said that I would return to the workplace after having kids, but now both kids are in school, and I am still here. What I didn't expect was that during that time I would forge a completely new identity as an artist and that I would start my own business from home. My primary responsibility was always caring for my kids, but as their independence grew, I used the new time to grow, and I came to realize that who I wanted to be was no longer who I had been.

The principal challenge with my choice, outside of the obvious treadmill of responsibilities, was loneliness. This was a common theme amongst the other artists who chose to stay at home, too. They used words like feeling "isolated, inadequate, and lonely." Rightly or wrongly, a lot of our self-validation does come from having a paycheque and being seen to be going to and returning from somewhere that needs us and where we have recognized responsibilities. When we give this up, we lose some of the things that we have in common with others and definitely many of the things that society perceives as being valuable. A few of us who chose to stay at home, myself included, felt this judgment directed at us from some working mothers, too, whether it was intentional or not.

Being with a baby or young child, you're lonely. You don't really have anyone to talk to, or at least you don't have anyone who will answer when you talk to them.

Trish Johnson

Life in a Bubble is my snapshot of my feelings about being a stay-at-home mother. One day in late winter while my son and I were out for a walk, I saw our reflection in a bubble in a frozen puddle. What I saw looked exactly like how I felt about my life at that point in time. For almost five years I had been at home with him, and for five years before that I had been home with his sibling. He and I were a little team each and every day, as connected as though the umbilical cord between us had never been cut. That feeling would be ending in a few short months when he would start school for the first time. That bubble captured the togetherness that we had, and reminded me that it would not always be this way.

At the same time, I also felt somewhat tethered, and definitely lonely. Although I always felt needed—sometimes asphyxiatingly so—and I was never ever physically alone, not even for a moment, I still felt alone. I was craving adult social interaction, but I had learned that the mommy groups were short lived. I met many other mother friends who were home with their children at different times, but by then almost all of them had filtered back to the workplace. I, however, was always at home. I didn't have an escape to think adult thoughts and to be with adult people. I had been out of the workforce for so long that I felt wholly removed from it; I felt between two worlds.

> **For all that your world can grow through having children, I have to be aware that is the best-case scenario; a woman's world can also shrink.**
>
> **Nadine Flagel**

> **For years, my husband would come home and I would go out. We had one car and he used it to go to work. Once my husband and the car came home, I went out to the local mall. I would get in the car about seven o'clock in the evening and heave a sigh of relief as I turned on CBC on the radio. Finally, a few spare moments to think my own thoughts.**
>
> **Trish Johnson**

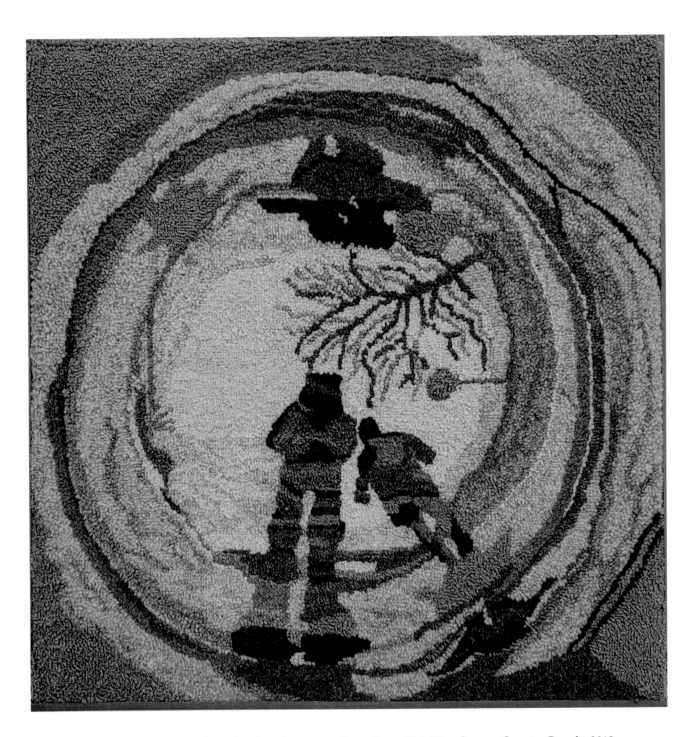

Life in a Bubble, 18" x 18", wool and acrylic yarns on linen. Karen D. Miller, Ottawa, Ontario, Canada, 2018.

So what does it all amount to in the end? Where do these choices lead us, and our identities as mothers? Three artists point the way forward for us. Amy Meissner shared what happened after she lost her sense of self after having her first child. She acknowledges that no woman is ever the same after having children. Importantly though, she points out that she has since regained an identity; it just isn't the one that she had before becoming a mother.

In *The Propagation of Daughters*, Michelle Kingdom further asserts that the vulnerability inherent in motherhood can lead to growth in your sense of self. In her piece, a once-dormant bulb sprouts upwards through the frosty earth to greet the arrival of spring. It represents the birth of her daughter, but also the way in which Michelle believes that she herself bloomed when she became a mother. Finally, Nadine Flagel (p. 47) discovered that "being vulnerable means you can hurt." But, and this is the critical point to me in all of this, "it also means you are able to change."

> **Nothing has overwhelmed me more than having my self become secondary to a small person. It was very liberating—there was so much joy in letting go of my ego, of being the everything for a tiny person. Of course, that initial, innate selfless intensity of motherhood faded over the years, and then I was seeking my self again, but as a different person.**
>
> **Sayward Johnson**

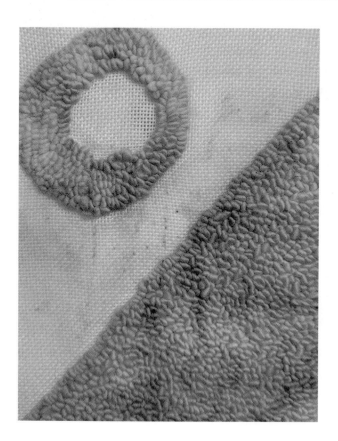

Marks of Motherhood VIII, 5" x 7," rust-dyed yarn on jute. Karen D. Miller, Ottawa, Ontario, Canada, 2017.

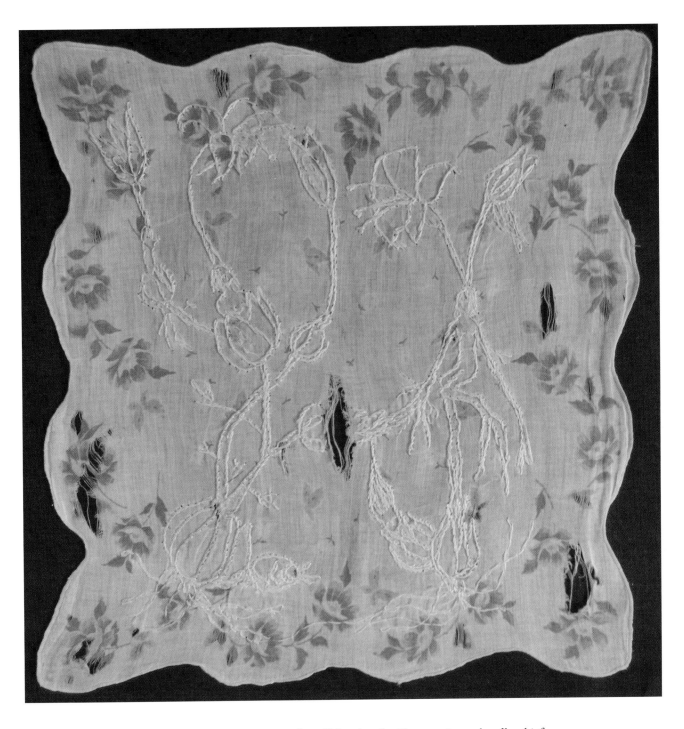

The Propagation of Daughters, 12" x 12", hand-embroidery on vintage handkerchief.
Michelle Kingdom, Burbank, California, USA, 2013.

4

All the Voices That We Have to Hear

I have a graduate degree in legal studies and so I have spent a lot of time in the academic trenches studying social structures and drivers of social change, such as parental leave legislation. I'm very used to how academics write. Now that I have been a mother for a few years, though, I have a lot less patience for it. I find terminology like "societal expectations" particularly insidious. It is a perfect example of how dispassionate academic writing ends up being, and how it can imbue fairly straightforward things with artificial—and harmful—import. It is absolutely true that societal expectations about motherhood are very real, and every mother suffers because of them, as we will see in this chapter. But what can we do about them? After all, what chance does any one woman stand against the mighty behemoth that is the society that is imposing these expectations?

Part of the answer, I suggest, lies in speaking plainly. Expectations are just opinions, and those opinions are held and expressed by everyday people. The thing is, you know some of those people, such as your family, friends, and workplace acquaintances. And your children are going to bring you into contact with a whole new world of health and education professionals, sports and recreation circles, and the like. You'll run into all kinds of people with just as many opinions about what is right, proper, and acceptable. If there is one thing that is true in this world, it is that everyone has an opinion, usually on everything.

Don't get me wrong, I'm not saying that it is easy to ignore expectations. After all, some of those opinions are expressed by people you know and love and whose respect you wish to keep. Life is full of such nuances. I confess that I struggled with these societal expectations precisely because I had spent my life up to then, like so many of us do, caring and minding what everybody that I met thought of me. When it came to motherhood, I certainly thought that I would make everyone happy, that indeed it was even my responsibility to do so, and that I had no choice but to be perfect at it.

Looking back, it is funny to think that I ever thought that way. That's the thing about societal expectations—they are so pervasive that you actually start to think that it is you who wants them! But something happened when I became a mother. By necessity, I had to determine what was really important, and in my case that meant some very difficult, personal, and long-overdue life decisions. After that, it was easier for me to see a lot of opinions for exactly what they were: just opinions. I realized that in fact not only did I have a choice in the face of the much-vaunted societal expectations, but in fact I had a great deal of it, and where I could, I took it. We will see from several stories in this chapter that others did, too.

> **Motherhood has left me open to all kinds of judgment.**
>
> **Michelle Kingdom**

Did I have all of the answers? Certainly not! In this chapter we will also see things that I and many others still struggle with. But, again, let's not fool ourselves that there is any mystery in this grandiose but opaque term "societal expectations." Let's just call it what it is, sexism in all of its forms, and then we'll know clearly what we are dealing with. After all, it is no coincidence that these expectations fall disproportionately on women.

Let's examine these societal expectations, and what we can do about them, more closely. To begin, I just love the title of Lori Laberge's piece *I'M OK*. In only two words, she expressed for me a core truth that every mother learns shortly after she gives birth. For nine months, at least for your first child, you are doted on and even fawned over. Doctors seem to monitor your every biological function. Your belly becomes a mystical thing that for some reason even perfect strangers think they might be entitled to rub. And then you give birth. People still ask how you are, but similar to when they ask "how are you doing?" on the street, it is only out of politeness. They don't actually want to be bothered by an answer. The polite and expected rejoinder is simply "I'm OK."

Lori's piece pulls back the veil on the reality behind the politesse. One of the biggest challenges that she faced as a mother of young children was feeling tired all the time, and the difficulties that arose from trying to function each day with little to no sleep. *I'M OK* highlights how the expectations of motherhood require women to not only alter their sleep patterns, but also to continue to keep up with everything—and do it all well. Symbolism abounds in this piece, from the medicine bottles which reference sleeping pills and energy pills, to a calendar chock-full of events to keep track of and a clock indicating the amount of time each day that goes into mothering. Lori definitely felt a "push and pull" throughout her mothering experiences; not just being pulled in many directions timewise, but also a struggle within herself. She believes that this struggle happens because mothers want so much for their children, but at the same time don't want to "lose themselves in the process." A single tear rolls down Lori's portrait, representing the sense of loss that she felt for the person that she used to be before she became a mother, and also the difficulty of raising children.

And yet, Lori's meaning with her title *I'M OK* is different than I initially took it. She means that, yes, in fact, in the end it is all going to be okay. This piece is a message of reassurance to new mothers that the feelings that they have are natural and that they will be fine. She even includes a motherhood award in her piece that she awards to all mothers, every one of whom earns it by making it through the motherhood journey.

We do need to have more intention about how we support new mothers. When asked, she'll say she's "great!" and "fine!" because that is what society dictates she's supposed to say, but look her in the eye and make sure.

Amy Meissner

I'M OK, 90" x 61", hand-dyed wool on linen, paint tarp, paper, gallon jars, prescription bottles, table, and photo prints.
Lori Laberge, Spruce Pine, North Carolina, USA, 2020.

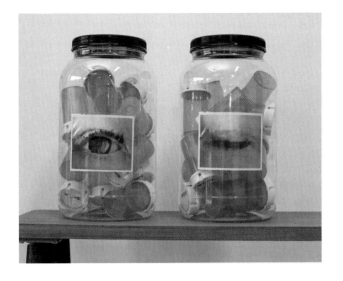

I'M OK (detail).

Be kind to yourself. Motherhood is a hard job and we have such high expectations for ourselves as mothers. Speak to yourself as you would a friend you love.

Meryl Cook

I think as mothers we need to be careful what we project to other mothers about what this is all supposed to look like. And while I didn't use much social media 12 years ago, I was still expecting blurry filters, white-washed walls, and dust motes. I was comparing my situation to something fictional. It's better to be reassured of the mess society handily pushes out of the frame so that we can keep it real.

Amy Meissner

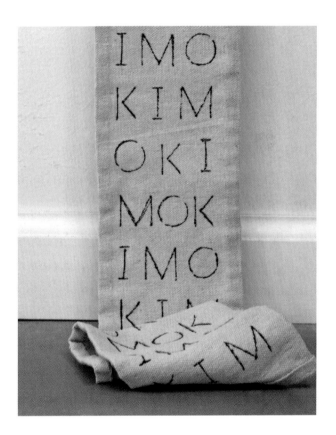

I'M OK (detail).

Perhaps nothing better illustrates society's expectations that mothers will always act like they are okay than women's experiences with postpartum depression. It is true that our understanding and recognition of this, and the treatment and support available for mothers suffering with it, has improved over the past few decades. But it is evident from many of the stories shared with me that even today there is still stigma and a lack of support when it comes to postpartum depression.

Midnight Madonna clearly shows Karen Larsen's love for her newborn son. But she also admits you to the darkness that she was feeling. Karen had her son in the 1970s. Postpartum depression wasn't a recognized illness then, but she knew that something didn't feel right. She portrays herself in dreary colours to reflect the depression that she says felt like being "in a deep dark hole." In contrast, her infant son lovingly cradled to her breast is "shiny, bright, and new."

Without access to medication or support, Karen was finally able to cope with what she was experiencing by talking to other women and joining a mother's group when her son was a toddler. Making *Midnight Madonna*, even all these years later, has also allowed her to reflect on that period of her life and to try to make sense of all of the feelings that she had. Karen now realizes that what she felt then wasn't wrong or unusual, but rather that she was just "experiencing things before they had a name."

Marks of Motherhood IX, 6" x 8", rust-dyed wool yarn, nylon stocking. Karen D. Miller, Ottawa, Ontario, Canada, 2020.

Midnight Madonna, 26.5" x 20.5", wool cloth strips, wool and acrylic yarns on linen.
Karen Larsen, Elliottsburg, Pennsylvania, USA, 2019.

Rachelle Leblanc was diagnosed with postpartum depression in the late 1990s, when her second daughter was eight months old. *Blue Dress* is a self-portrait of that painful period of her life. In making this very personal piece, Rachelle explains that "thoughts of how tired I was, how crazy I felt, and the feelings of harming myself are transferred into each loop." The challenge of the illness was made worse for Rachelle by the stigma and misunderstanding that she felt from those around her. Unlike Karen, Rachelle had access to medication, but she felt criticized for taking it and spent her days in a blur of conflicting emotions: "dazed, drugged, exhausted, lonely, happy, and content all at the same time." She felt intense pressure to just smile and shake off her depression, as if it were something that she could control.

Five butterflies, representing the age of her daughter when Rachelle finally began to feel normal again, soar above this self-portrait, indicating what she says is the "power of personal transformation." Although it is a deeply personal and difficult subject for her, Rachelle feels it is important to talk about that time in her life as "those who are trying to be the perfect moms need to know that we are all the same." Rachelle is aware of a number of women who were feeling alone and who found comfort in hearing her story and, for her, that makes it all the easier to speak her truth.

Even when I had postpartum, I would tell myself this is perfection. You may not feel that way, but you need to remember this. You are happy.

Rachelle Leblanc

Those moments of numbness, forgetfulness, desperation, and loneliness can envelop one's every thought.

Rachelle Leblanc

Blue Dress, 45" x 14" x 8", cashmere, wool on linen, cotton thread, linen, polyester fill, wood, earthenware, medium fire glaze, and nichrome wire. Rachelle Leblanc, Katy, Texas, USA, 2016.

After waiting a long time to have children and arming herself with numerous parenting books, Amy Meissner thought that she had prepared herself fully for motherhood and would be "really good at it, probably perfect, actually." So when she developed postpartum depression, anxiety, and obsessive compulsive tendencies that lingered after her children became toddlers, Amy felt a mixture of both disappointment and guilt. She knew intuitively that she should be happy because, after all, both of her children were healthy and she had a supportive husband. Yet she was "still a mess" and was "intolerant of my own weaknesses and spent time berating myself."

Amy represents that dark and miserable time period in *Descent*. The black form suspended above the colourful field below is symbolic of her postpartum depression, an object that "feels foreign, alien, burning its way through a pristine landscape that—as women, as mothers—we've been promised and therefore expected." Amy now recognizes that the guilt she felt, and the way that she treated herself then, was unlike how she would treat either her children or her spouse. But, she says, women "find it difficult to nurture and protect the self."

> **It took a long time before I could emerge—altered—from this decimated and disappointing landscape.**
>
> **Amy Meissner**

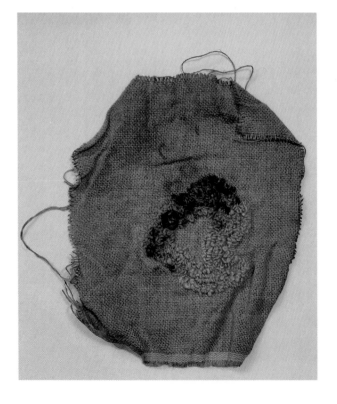

Marks of Motherhood X, 11.5" x 9.5, rust-dyedwool yarns onlinen. Karen D. Miller, Ottawa, Ontario, Canada, 2021.

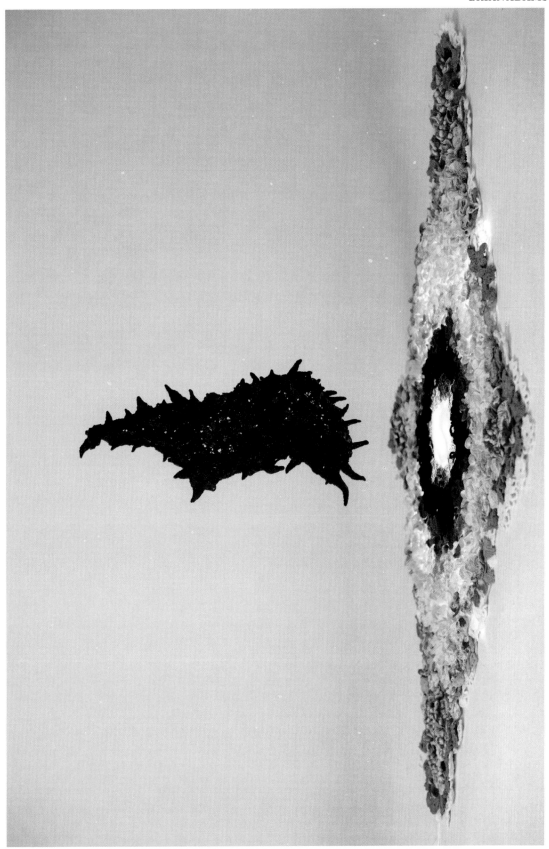

Descent, 35" x 53" (suspended component 20" x 9" x 9"), vintage doilies, silk organza, rubber, wire, epoxy clay, and light. Amy Meissner, Anchorage, Alaska, USA, 2017.

When looking at *Antidote* by Nadine Flagel, you could be forgiven if you assumed that it is just a cheerful depiction of colourful flowers. There is, in fact, much more to it. After giving birth to her first son, Nadine endured a difficult postpartum adjustment. She was angry towards her partner and had "intrusive thoughts," insomnia, and heightened anxiety. She found it very difficult to admit to her partner that she was struggling because she felt that she was already asking him for so much. Perhaps even more importantly, she wasn't even really sure what to ask for.

During this time, Nadine struggled to work on this piece because she found it difficult to concentrate and focus on the work. But she did finish it, and she named it *Antidote*, a name with a number of very personal meanings for her. It has become a symbol for her of how she "was able to push back against the thoughts that parenthood was poison" and that parenthood was "wholly detrimental to a woman's sense of well-being and worth."

Nadine also always thought of the flowers in the piece as poppies, which for her are "a personal symbol of pharmaceuticals." Completing this piece symbolized that she "accepted without judgment the regular contribution of medication" in creating and maintaining balance in her mental health. Working on this piece was itself a form of creative antidote for her postpartum depression. It and her medication were ways that Nadine took "responsibility for and worked towards feeling better about motherhood."

As with all other aspects of motherhood, support for women suffering from postpartum depression is key. Nadine was fortunate to find a support group of women in her area who understood what she was going through. For Nadine, "saying the worst thing in my head and then seeing other people nod or hearing them speak about a similar feeling can be such a powerful reminder of one's essential worthiness to be part of the community."

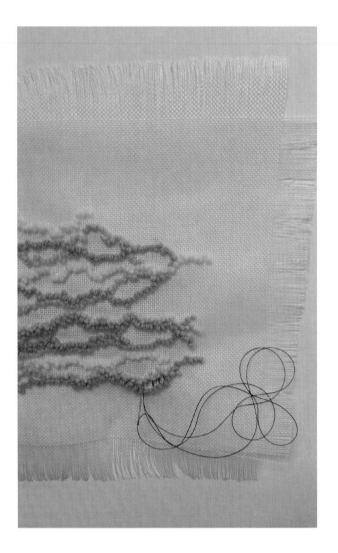

Marks of Motherhood XI (detail), 11" x 14", wool yarn and thread on jute. Karen D. Miller, Ottawa, Ontario, Canada, 2021.

Antidote, 32" x 32", recycled wool on linen. Based on an art nouveau design by Rene Beauclair.
Nadine Flagel, Vancouver, British Columbia, Canada, 2007.

The complex thing about expectations is that, as with everything in life, they are a mix of positive and negative. The trick is in the balance. Take our own appearance, for one example. We all want to be beautiful, and especially to truly feel beautiful. It would even be nice if our partners occasionally acknowledged that we are.

The problem is that when it comes to beauty, far too much of that perception is out of our hands. Because whatever we are going through, mothers are still women, and in our society that is still rife with sexual objectification and the ideal of eternal youth. We women know all too well how we are expected to keep up our appearances, no matter how we feel or how busy we get.

But motherhood is messy. It definitely takes a toll on our bodies. The artists in this book list numerous physical changes that have come along with being a mother, both from giving birth and afterward. None of these ever appear on the tabloid covers in the supermarket checkout line or on our social media feeds: morning sickness, c-section scars, tearing, infections, weight gain, stress-induced hair loss, back pain, herniated disks, and certainly not leaky bladders. To say that this is a problem of two different realities still misses the point; in fact, it is the impossibility of reconciling reality and fantasy.

In What She's Having, Alexandrya Eaton takes a colourful pop-art approach to the pressure that women and mothers feel to always be "perfect and beautiful." Where does this pressure come from? There is no great mystery in that. Alexandrya points to television, magazines, and social media, but also, disappointingly, it comes from other women.

Alexandrya points out how these expectations go beyond our own appearance, extending to the pressure of perfection in everything that we do. We know this, too. We know that no matter what else is going on, any perceived issues in the outward appearance of our family, our house, or our careers are seen as our shortcomings. When her children were younger, Alexandrya remembers feeling like she was always rushing but never getting ahead, and "never doing enough."

As Alexandrya herself has aged, she has come to the welcome realization that the unrelenting expectations to be perfect and beautiful are unrealistic. Being unattainable, they can only ever leave you feeling that you are somehow inadequate. This is the perfect recipe for unhappiness. Alexandyra is much happier since she learned to let those expectations go and to care less about what others think.

> **My body changed more in just a few months than it had in the previous twenty years.**
>
> **Nadine Flagel**

What She's Having, 30" x 60", wool on burlap. Alexandrya Eaton, Sackville, New Brunswick, Canada, 2020.

The expectation that mothers will sacrifice their own interests is another complicated issue. Because that is exactly what we do—and often very much what we want to do—for our children.

But in uniformly wanting women to do everything and to be everything, society doesn't really think anything through. Its expectations are unsophisticated and simplistic so—unsurprisingly—it starts to trip over itself when confronted with uncomfortable realities. Unfortunately, this sends harmful messages to women who are just trying to do the right thing.

Take single motherhood, for example. Patti Colen divorced when divorce was still "fairly taboo." In addition to having to navigate her own emotions around the now "broken view" of what she had thought "motherhood, parenting, and my life would be," she also had to deal with judgment from those around her. She was keenly aware that as the woman, any breakdown of the family was seen as her fault. She knew that the expectation on her as the mother was that she would sacrifice her own happiness and stay in the relationship for the sake of her child. It would be wonderful to be able to say today that this antiquated and misguided point of view has been consigned to history to the benefit of everyone involved, but unfortunately, we all know that that isn't true at all. In Patti's experience, the expectations weren't just put on her. She knew that those around her were also judging her young daughter for being from a "broken home," only further contributing to her feelings of "inadequacy."

Seeing that society's expectations for her and her daughter were unhelpful, and even potentially destructive, Patti had to be that much stronger in order to successfully plot her own course. She knew that she had to find the right path that would ensure that her daughter would "not be another statistic" and, further, would shield her from the harmful effects of blind stigma. *Reconstructing Childhood* uses the imagery of a jigsaw puzzle, representing how Patti saw her family broken into different pieces with the divorce, and her resulting focus on having to put the pieces back together in a new way that would work for both her and her daughter. Some of the pieces of the puzzle were more of a struggle to place than others. For example, Patti didn't pursue any new romantic relationships for a very long time, afraid of the possible effect on her daughter if they didn't work out. However, even though there were a lot of difficult moments in putting the puzzle together, Patti still chose to depict a mother looking lovingly at her daughter because for her the challenges "of motherhood, especially as a single mother, are worth every minute."

Reconstructing Childhood, 20" x 29.5", hand-dyed wool and yarns on linen. Patti Colen, London, Ontario, Canada, 2021.

Even the reality of the relentless physical and mental demands of motherhood are, like everything else, neither absolutely good nor bad.

To be clear, these demands are real, as Emily van Lidth de Jeude graphically depicts in *Maternity Wear*. She shows that the obligations of mothering are "all-encompassing," and further that once a woman gives birth, "her body isn't her body anymore." Instead, from then on there is always someone "pulling, sucking, and needing her." We are fully aware of this, and we know that we don't have infinite reserves of energy and strength to give. Yet many women are still surprised to realize that somewhere along the line, it all becomes too much. Then, we can feel our own gang of toddlers that Emily has painted climbing up the train of her wedding dress, and we can understand the mother who is "frantically trying to escape through the torn bodice and get out of the garment of motherhood."

How can the burdens of our own hectic lives, the very lives that we live in their full minutiae every single day, creep up on us like this? Emily explains the paradox, and in so doing points the way to recovery. First, we carry our children inside of us for nine months and we commit ourselves to the "weight of their burden." Then, precisely because we are so full of love for them, we give ourselves away to them. Even though we know that this comes with a cost, it can still feel effortless, particularly at first. However, as the cliché goes, motherhood is a marathon, not a sprint. It is when we keep giving ourselves away without refuelling that giving ourselves away becomes a "burden."

When it becomes overwhelming, we need to find a way to get away and "feel in ourselves again." Emily describes this as putting aside our guilt and "taking off the dress" so that we can find the necessary balance between "giving away and giving to ourselves." We can put the dress back on, so to speak, when we are regrounded and ready.

And that, for many of us, is what we do want. As Emily points out, feeling needed is also quite "validating." Speaking for myself, sure, when everybody's eyes always turn to you because they know your husband hasn't a clue, it can sometimes be tedious. But more often, yes, thanks for recognizing who is in charge around here.

Maternity Wear (detail), 60" x 72" (oval footprint is 84"), reclaimed wedding gown, acrylic paint, reclaimed pacifiers, dressmaking findings, and other reclaimed fabric. Emily van Lidth de Jeude, Bowen Island/Nex̱wlélex̱m British Columbia, Canada, 2018.

Maternity Wear, 60" x 72" (oval footprint is 84"), reclaimed wedding gown, acrylic paint, reclaimed pacifiers, dressmaking findings, and other reclaimed fabric. Emily van Lidth de Jeude, Bowen Island/Neᶻwlélexm British Columbia, Canada, 2018.

This next piece is critically important to me because it exposes an assumption that I have been making all the way through this book up until now. I have been implicitly assuming that all mothers have the same basic capacities to mother and face the same barriers. Of course, this isn't true at all. Just like everybody else in society, mothers get no exemptions from, for example, the implacable limitations imposed on them from poverty or from discrimination for the colour of their skin or their sexual orientation.

Another such implacable limitation is physical disability. It might be managed, but it is never going away. It means that for every challenge that a mother faces about what to do, she always faces one more on top of that: how?

With These Hands is my work, but it was inspired by my friend Laurie, who has had rheumatoid arthritis since she was a teenager. The hands in the piece are her hands, photographed and then enlarged into two three-dimensional sculptures. She is the mother of two children the same ages as my own, and since becoming a mother she has had two major surgeries. Additionally, to manage the chronic pain of her disease she is always dealing with medications that bring particularly unhelpful side effects, like fatigue.

This is not at all my experience, so I asked her whether or not she feels there is extra pressure on her to meet all of the expectations that are placed on mothers. Her answer was an unequivocal "yes." She acknowledged that many times her body does not allow her to keep up with what other parents are doing, and she often feels judged for that because fatigue is "invisible and very hard to explain to people."

Though I think I am a pretty good problem solver, I appreciate that Laurie has to function at a whole different level just to do even the smallest things that I don't have to think about. Because of the limited use of her hands, for example, Laurie had to find new ways to carry her children, to open baby food jars, and to fasten onesies, amongst countless other things. As Laurie points out, though, this level of ingenuity and adaptability is often overlooked.

The amount of pain that Laurie deals with every day also has other effects on her mothering experience. Pain, as we can all appreciate, inevitably affects your mood. The chronic pain that Laurie lives with makes it more difficult to focus, but she always has to fight through it. After all, she still needs to be mom to her kids and to be there for their needs, and that is just as perpetual. As the years pass and her children grow older, she does feel sadness about the activities that she is just not able to do with them.

> **I think a lot of mothers—whether they are able-bodied or not—have this expectation of what they should be doing as a mother. When you don't fit into this mould, it's stressful and means renegotiating who you are as a mom.**
>
> **Laurie Proulx**

My intention with *With These Hands* was to bring attention to the phenomenal strength and perseverance that mothers demonstrate out of deep love for their children. But I'll leave the last word on this to Laurie who says that: "In some ways, I wish society would stop looking at people with disabilities as a burden to live with and saw how we actually bring a lot to the table to all parts of life."

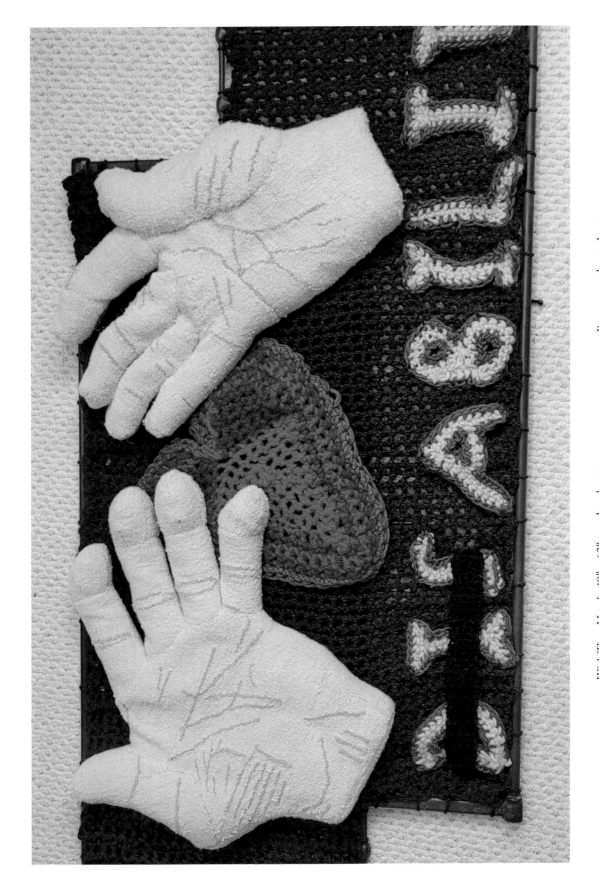

With These Hands, 49" x 62", wool and cotton yarns on rug warp, acrylic yarn, and metal gates.
Karen D. Miller, Ottawa, Ontario, Canada, 2020.

The greatest problem with being constantly pressured to meet unattainable expectations is the consequences to us. Despite our strength, and regardless of our intentions to ignore them, they are like heavy rain on a leaky roof. Eventually the water seeps through our defenses and wreaks havoc on our already vulnerable insides. We feel compelled to defend ourselves, to respond even when it isn't practical. We overwhelm ourselves trying to satisfy a standard that we don't agree with, and we feel insufficient and guilty when we inevitably fail. These themes come up over and over again in art that is honest about motherhood.

"Mama, what in this house can catch on fire?" was a question that Amy Meissner's then four-year-old son posed to her. She responded by listing all of the things in their home that were particularly flammable. But the more she thought about it, the more she realized that the one thing in their home that was most likely to spontaneously combust was in fact . . . herself. Trying to keep up with all of the responsibilities and expectations of her new role as a mother had left Amy feeling overwhelmed. She experienced an "explosion of history, of motherhood, of the demands of children, of the expectations of other women, of her identity and its loss, and finally, its regain." Realizing that she was the thing "spontaneously combusting" made her ashamed, but creating *Spontaneous Combustion* allowed her to deal with those "uncomfortable" feelings in a tangible way. *Spontaneous Combustion* invites us to discuss those feelings that society tells us we shouldn't feel or talk about. As mothers, we have to realize that we are not alone. We'll look at this in more depth in the next chapter.

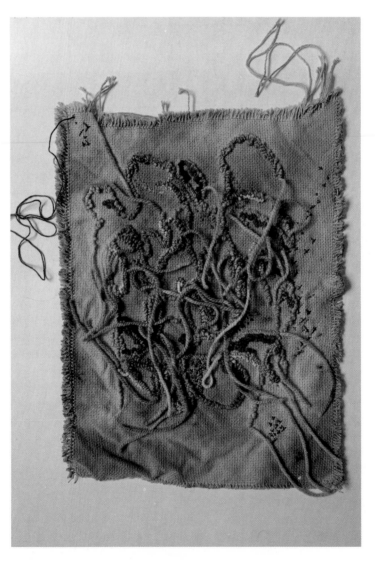

Marks of Motherhood XII, 16" x 12", rust-dyed yarns and wool yarns on rug warp.
Karen D. Miller, Ottawa, Ontario, Canada, 2021.

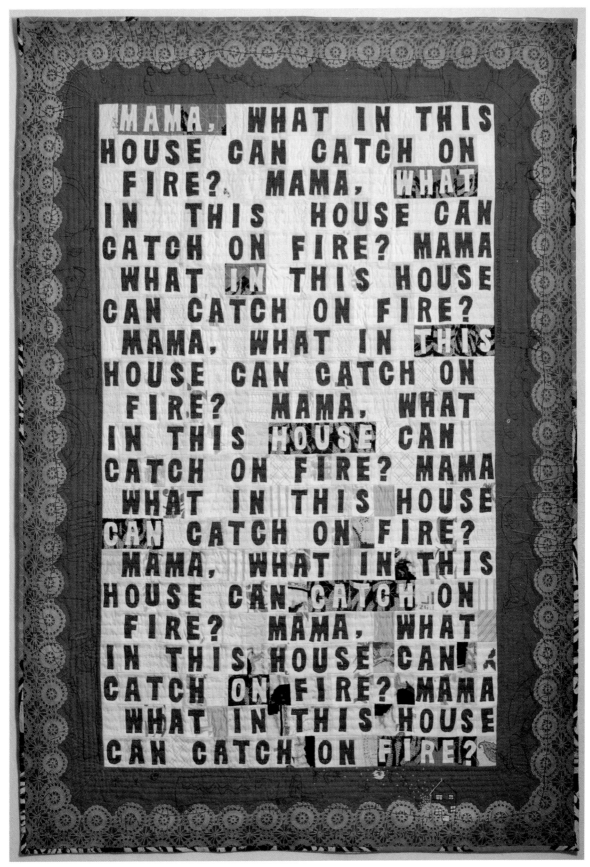

Spontaneous Combustion, 77" x 54", wool, cotton, and vintage domestic linens; machine pieced, hand embroidered, hand appliquéd, and hand quilted. Amy Meissner, Anchorage, Alaska, USA, 2013.

Technical Study: Motherhood in Art

Motherhood Still Life #2: The Living Room (detail), 38.5" x 30.5", wool yarns and acrylic yarns, acrylic paint on linen. Karen D. Miller, Ottawa, Ontario, Canada, 2019.

Chances are, if you were asked to name five famous artists off the top of your head, almost all of them would be male. Why is that? Were there no women artists? Of course, there were. Women have been making art for centuries, but for the most part have not gained the same notoriety and prominence as their male counterparts. This is partly because for centuries, women were excluded from the art academies and schools, and were not able to pursue art as a profession.

There were exceptions to this, such as Italian painter Artemisia Gentileschi (1593–1656) who learned in her father's painting studio. But for the most part, the annals of art history have ignored women's contributions to the art world, if they even acknowledged that such contributions existed at all. The expansion of women's legal rights over time and the gradual acceptance of formal education for women eventually led to opportunities for women to pursue art as a career. But even so, biases in the art world persisted long afterwards and so many female artists signed their work with just their initials in order to avoid prejudice. As a result, there has long been gender imbalance in favour of males in the representation of artists in gallery exhibitions and collections. This is starting to change, and some galleries are now committing to greater equity in the shows that they put on and the work that they acquire. However, the art that we as a society generally consider to be the most valuable in both monetary and cultural terms is still largely the art created by men.

It is no surprise, then, that although motherhood has been a theme in art since antiquity, for a long time it was from the male perspective, as seen from the outside looking in and seeing what they wanted to see. In the beginning, motherhood was depicted with reference to religious icons and saintly images of the Madonna and Christ Child. It was not until the eighteenth century that there began to be more intimate portraits made of mothers and their children, but again the scenes tended to be idealized and romanticized. And they tended to be painted mostly by men, with a few exceptions, such as the work of French painter Élisabeth Vigée Le Brun (1755–1842), known for her portraits of Marie Antoinette and her children.

Scenes more familiar to us today began to appear in the art world in the nineteenth century. American painter Mary Cassatt (1844–1926) was one of the most notable artists exploring the theme of maternity at that time. Even though she did not have children of her own, she began to depict scenes from the everyday life of real women and their children and their relationship to one another. Contemporary artists have taken the subject of motherhood even further and are exploring the physical, mental, and emotional consequences of having children.

These artists are calling into question the societal expectations placed on mothers and whether or not mothers can, or should, "do it all."

Galleries have not always created space for art that explores the theme of motherhood, perhaps because the artists were women, or perhaps because these real images don't portray the ideal of motherhood that society has held on to for so long. Even today, there is still a stigma attached to being a mother in the art world, and women often feel that they are presented with a choice: be an artist or be a mother. Male artists, on the other hand, tend not to have to contemplate whether having children will hurt their art careers. But things are slowly beginning to change. There are more and more mother artist groups emerging, providing support and exhibition opportunities for mother artists. As well, there are now dedicated artist residencies for parents and art prizes dedicated to artists who are mothers. In time, I hope that artists who are also mothers will be invited to embrace this core element of their identity and life experience as a means of furthering their career options and opportunities.

In addition to the artists contributing to this book, here are some examples of other artists, past and present, who depict motherhood in their work:

- Berthe Morisot
- Louise Bourgeois
- Mary Pratt
- Christiane Pflug
- Mary Cassatt
- Paula Modersohn-Becker
- Katherine Duclos
- Ruth de Vos
- Natalie Bruvels

Motherhood Still Life #3: Nude Study (detail), 26.5" x 38", wool and acrylic yarns on linen.
Karen D. Miller, Ottawa, Ontario, Canada, 2020.

5

Taking Control

What can we really do about expectations? As I have said, the first modest step is honesty: with each other, with ourselves, and with those around us. Motherhood, for all of its blessings and wonder, is a job, and at times is a relentlessly monotonous one. The efficiency of a sound routine saves us, and it also stultifies us. When I walk into the kitchen some mornings, my dread of making school lunches is all out of proportion to the task. It weighs on me not because it is any great trial, but precisely because it is so trivial, and because I know that hundreds of my mornings ahead are going to play out in exactly the same way. I spoke earlier about choices, and an important choice is to accept your own feelings about what you are living. After all, only then can you exercise any control over your own life by making choices about what to do about what you are feeling.

We have to acknowledge that motherhood, like any job, has dualities. If we are at the office and we detest the routine of filing expense reports or explaining our last quarter to the boss, we are more naturally inclined to just do it and move on. If we feel underappreciated or worth more, we are more accustomed to being vocal about it. It should be the same with motherhood, but for many of us, it isn't. Unfortunately, we don't permit ourselves to voice those all-too-human irritations because we think that somehow it's selfish and reflects poorly on our love for our children, or that it means that we are somehow ungrateful for their presence. Of course, none of that bears up to any scrutiny. Nothing about the less-glamorous realities of motherhood—and which realities of motherhood, exactly, are glamorous?—negates the wonder of what you are doing and the happiness it gives you. You chose to be a mother, but you never vowed to be a saint. Your feelings are real, and like any feelings, you need to acknowledge them. There is nothing wrong with that.

Not Your Doormat is my own rather self-explanatory way of voicing my own such feelings. We as women, and especially as mothers, often feel something akin to a doormat. Our contributions to our households and to our family's lives are many, but they often go unnoticed, unappreciated, and come to be expected. In a somewhat different approach to the traditional welcome mat, my piece is full of almost 500 pins. No one would want to walk across or wipe their feet on this mat. It is my unsubtle announcement to society and its expectations that my work as a mother has value. It deserves to be noticed and appreciated just as much as any paid employment.

Not Your Doormat (detail), 18" x 31", cotton fabric, acrylic yarn on linen. Karen D. Miller, Ottawa, Ontario, Canada, 2021.

Not Your Doormat, 18" x 31", cotton fabric, acrylic yarn on linen. Karen D. Miller, Ottawa, Ontario, Canada, 2021.

A number of the contributors to this book have already pointed out the high long-term value to mothers of just stepping away and taking time for themselves. I can hear the groans and the laughter now. Time? Who has any of that?

Because isn't that the deep irony of society's expectations? At the same time that women are told that motherhood is their ultimate life goal, where are all of the supports to help us carry out this role? Where, for example, is the reliable childcare so that women who want to pursue a professional life can do so without having to worry about their children's basic daily needs? Where is the flexibility in workplace arrangements so that all of the day-to-day tasks, such as school drop-offs and pickups, taking days off from work when their children are ill, and taking leave to take kids to appointments, don't always disproportionately fall on mothers? Where, indeed, is acknowledgment of the emotional labour of mothers in the home and in the workplace, and the acknowledgment of all of the labour that goes into mothering? Where, in all of the legislation that governs us, is the recognition of the need for equality in the physical, emotional, and mental division of labour between mothers and fathers? Honestly, if we should be laughing ruefully about anything, it's that.

So, we're on our own to make our way through a world that wants children, but wants even more to be spared the details.

We need to find our own support networks. Even there, we face long odds. Many contributors to this book, myself included, had a spouse or partner who travelled extensively for their work, or worked such long hours that they might as well have been travelling. Family was often too far away to help. Others, such as military spouses, moved so frequently that developing reliable social networks was at best a hit-or-miss affair. So, we try as best as we can, through our circle of friends, through childcare groups, whatever we can. Because as laughably impossible a task as it is, we all understand that we need to take care of ourselves, because if we don't, there will be nothing left to give to care for our children.

I don't have any magic answer to this question. But I can say that art was part of the answer for me. Not at the beginning, of course, when at best the end of the day left me only able to stare blankly at a wall with a glass of wine and wonder what it was like to be able to think. But as time passes and your children grow, then the pockets of time do emerge, and the scope for choice reemerges. Art met many of my needs then, and still does today.

> My sister and I helped each other. Because we had no mother to help us, we tried to help each other.
>
> **Trish Johnson**

Working on my art is my way of making space for myself.

Art for me was my therapy through self-care. The greatest advantage of self-care is that you are in charge. You know better than anyone what you need most in the random ten minutes that you might have, so it is entirely your own choice how to go about giving yourself the therapy that you most need. For many of the artists who contributed to this book, that outlet was through art, and specifically through fibre art. It didn't do any of the laundry, it didn't put any food on the table, and it didn't console the crying child, but it did give us a precious few moments to step off of that treadmill, forget it all for just a little bit, and come back surprisingly reenergized.

Many of the artists in this book told me that self-care was not something that was often modelled to them by their own mothers and so it did not come naturally to them, but they came to understand its value. For Lori Laberge, entering her studio each day where she could focus on her art and leave everything else "on the other side of the door" was something she always looked forward to. It took Emily van Lidth de Jeude many years before she could feel comfortable leaving her kids with someone else for short periods of time. She started reaching for creativity as a means to escape, first by heading into the woods with her camera in hand, and then eventually moving to art-making in her studio. As her children have grown, she still feels needed but says that the burden is smaller now, and she feels better equipped to take breaks when she needs to.

> **Our children actually benefit from seeing us meet our own needs—even when that requires us taking a break from mothering for a short time. When they see us feed our own souls, they learn to feed theirs, and that, after all, is what we hope for.**
>
> **Emily van Lidth de Jeude**

> **It's like that old adage that you need to put on your life vest first. I believe that unless we come to our lives with a sense of what we need in order to be happy and healthy—as moms, partners, artists, friends, daughters, and so much more—we won't be available for anyone else.**
>
> **Carmen Bohn**

I began creating hooked fibre art when my first child was just a baby. I would sneak away to my frame to pull a few loops during naptime. Given all of the interruptions that mothers face in a day, this artistic work felt like a good fit for me. There was nothing that I needed to keep track of or count; I could pick it up and put it down at a moment's notice. When her children were small, Alexandrya Eaton moved from painting to rug hooking as it was something that she could do from home rather than having to arrange for care so she could go to her painting studio. Another benefit of fibre art for her, I would imagine, is not having to keep little hands out of her paints! Amy Meissner found her way back to textile work when she became a mother because it was something that she could "easily manipulate with small children at her feet." She found this arrangement conducive to motherhood and pursuing a creative life, though she admits that she is still constantly striving for balance between the two.

> **Working by hand has been my stand-in for meditation, and I happen to have a deep commitment to this craft. I find it vital and necessary for my mental health, and therefore place a lot of value on this act and this skill.**
>
> **Amy Meissner**

Beyond the practicalities of meshing fibre art with little beings, many of the artists speak of there being something more to it. When Nadine Flagel first became a mother, she found it difficult to focus enough to rug hook. She gravitated instead to knitting and found that the tactile contact and repetitive motions of that craft were therapeutic. Once she felt ready to pick up her piece, *Antidote* (p. 47), and complete it, she said that working on it allowed her to be "present and outside herself" and to "feel good in her body."

Others said that the slower processes of fibre art are more conducive to meditation and relaxation than other art forms. For others who were struggling with their feelings, the act of pulling individual loops in their rug hooking allowed them to process their thoughts and transfer their feelings into their work. Working on her piece, *William* (p. 99), allowed Jane Smith to feel con-

nected to her son. In fact, to some extent Jane didn't want to complete the piece as she knew that this would mean the end of the tactile connection that she was experiencing. Amy Meissner found that her textile work gave her an opportunity to counter some of the frustrations she was feeling as a mother of young children, and for her "the repetition of line after line and stitch after stitch was a way to temper the monotony with a skill I still possessed."

I will close with one more point in favour of fibre art as a realistic avenue of self therapy: cost. I'm sure that many who read the last few pages will be put off by the references to studios, and probably the cost of the equipment and the materials. I know that many mothers have to struggle to find every dollar for their kids' needs, and the concept of an extra dollar for themselves—let alone a studio!—is as foreign as Mars. These are accomplished, and in many cases fully professional, artists, so please do not be put off by that. The practice of fibre art is quite different and very accessible.

Hooking requires exceptionally little in terms of either training, materials, equipment, space, or time. If you haven't tried hooking before, you can learn in minutes. For equipment, you need only a hook to pull loops; the hook I learned on looked like it was just a bent nail. For materials, many artists are going back to the roots of the art form and using repurposed materials. Any material with an open weave can be used as a backing, and any cloth that can be cut or torn can be turned into strips to hook. I teach my beginner classes on small plastic embroidery hoops, but any method that keeps your backing taut enough to pull loops through it will do. The whole project can be tucked away in a shopping bag when you aren't working on it. And most importantly for any mother, preparation time is almost nil; it takes only seconds to pick up from where you left off and carry on.

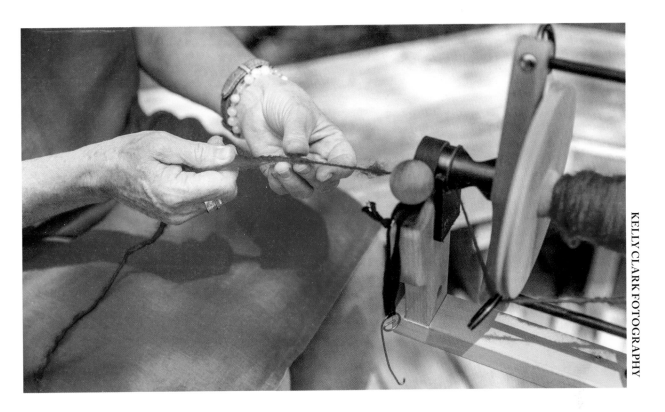

Meryl Cook spinning yarn.

I am a fibre artist. Working with fibres connects me to my art. I love the feel of the fibres as they move through my hands and fingers. Perhaps a painter feels this connection from her hand to her paintbrush and to the bristles that move the paint. I don't know.

Meryl Cook

6

Mother, Mother

It is not the Middle Ages anymore. In those times, your mother would have passed down to you all the skills that you needed to be a mother yourself. You would have modelled all of your own mothering after her, and perhaps also those in her close circle.

Today, for better or for worse, we have a much wider world to pattern ourselves after, a world filled with more than enough voices to advise us on what to do. Still, we were all children once, and for those years our own mothers were the North Stars that we looked to as we grew into the world. It is no wonder then that even in this, the modern world, our gratitude and regrets for what our own mothers taught us comes up so often in our art about motherhood. Wherever she is, she shapes us still.

Obviously, our own mothering shapes us, too, as we so internalize the hopes and dreams of our children that we might even start to think they are our own dreams. This much we all have in common: we all want the very best for our children, whatever that might look like and however it might change, for so long as we breathe. We want them to be happy, and from the youngest age we look forward to sharing those things with them that hold special memories for us. For me it was taking them on trips to my favourite places in the world, making them my most delicious family recipes, and showing them all kinds of things that I had done as a child. I could have made a whole book on this aspect alone because we are very good at telling these stories.

But what if you are one of the many mothers who doesn't look back on your own childhood with unmitigated fondness? If you remember your own mother struggling with certain challenges, then how she dealt with them stays with you, and one way or another it affects your own choices. If you are being honest with yourself, there is probably always something that you saw your mother do that you said to yourself, "I will never do that when I have kids!" If you are still being honest with yourself, you will probably admit that there were many things about your mother's choices that you only understood years later. And there will be choices that you kept your word about and never made, because you felt something then that she didn't see, or that she chose not to see.

All women have feelings of doubt and anxiety when they become mothers, but for Elizabeth Miller those feelings were intensified by the complex trauma she experienced as a child. Not having been raised with "patience, tolerance, or much freedom," she wasn't really sure how to give that to her own children, and particularly her two eldest sons. Once Elizabeth recognized her initial, unconscious tendency to repeat some of the mistakes made by her own parents, she learned to adopt the attitude: "This stops with this generation." This drove Elizabeth to make parenting choices that were different from what she had herself experienced as a child, replacing judgment and control with acceptance and self-determination for her boys.

In *Breaking the Cycle*, Elizabeth uses the imagery of a staircase, with a mother figure on either side looking on and centering her children in the middle. The bottom steps contain negative words which represent the trauma that she experienced as a child because Elizabeth says that she figuratively "tripped up the steps" while raising her sons but was "tripping over herself nonetheless" because of the lasting impact of her own childhood. Eventually, though, she reached the top of the steps, which contain positive words representing the joys, difficulties, and "willing sacrifices" she made for her boys, and she believes that being a mother played a large role in making her "whole again." Although her piece is very personal, Elizabeth hopes that it will allow other mothers to think about what their staircase words might be and to reflect on their own motherhood journey. While some aspects of motherhood are universal, Elizabeth believes that every single path is different and that no mother "climbs the staircase unscathed, but in the ascent she personally discovered as much about herself as she did about the young men she had the privilege to raise."

Breaking the Cycle, 18" x 24", hand-dyed wool, yarns, taffeta, stretch velvet, and green gems on linen.
Elizabeth Miller, Paris, Maine, USA, 2021.

I want to introduce this next artist, and the role of *Mother Me* in this story, very carefully. It is an instructive case that requires the telling of an extreme situation to illustrate the vast power that you have as a mother to do good for your children and the world, and especially good that you yourself may never have been accorded.

Linda Friedman Schmidt's mother spent all of her pivotal teen years in fear, running from the Nazis during World War II. When the war ended, her mother married and quickly became pregnant with Linda. Unfortunately, Linda's mother was so traumatized that, as Linda tells it, what her mother really needed at that point was "nurturing herself." She was certainly not ready for the selflessness required for either marriage or motherhood.

So, when Linda was born in a displaced persons camp in Germany, it isn't hard for us to imagine how challenging this situation would have been for even the strongest, most committed of us. With no close family around to support her, Linda's mother became "depressed" and was "disconnected and emotionally unavailable." Unfortunately, Linda says that it is extremely common amongst such "survivor mothers" to be unable to fully connect emotionally with their children. Linda observed that her mother did not enjoy motherhood, and transparently went through the motions of providing for Linda's basic needs. Linda had food and clothing, but nothing more. Linda, in turn, did not feel safe, secure, loved, or that she belonged. She felt very lonely and unhappy.

I feel as though I've come toward the top of the motherhood staircase with metaphorical banged-up knees and stubbed toes as I've sometimes failed in my vision of what a mother should be, occasionally falling back in to patterns I was raised with.

Elizabeth Miller

Mother Me, 44" x 40", discarded clothing and blankets. Linda Friedman Schmidt, New York Metro Area, USA, 2006.

But it is not true, despite what some people think, that what happens to the child preordains what the adult will become. Our mothers shape us, but they do not make us. That is not in any way to suggest that Linda's motherhood journey was easy. It was not. Her biggest challenge was to fight the compulsion to repeat the experiences of her childhood with her own children. She had to deliberately take the opposite approach. She happily devoted as much time as she could to her girls: talking to them, reading to them, playing games with them, and showing them the love and safety that she herself never received because her own mother was suffering. Becoming a mother was, for Linda, a liberation of sorts, when "the part of me that is like a little child, the part that was stifled in my own childhood, finally had a chance to come out to play."

In recent years, as the character of my children has solidified and I can begin to see the adults that they will become, I have begun to experience that special worry that makes those mothers who came before me laugh and tell me emphatically that it never goes away. What kind of world have I brought them into? Will they be okay? Have I taught them enough, well enough, that they will adapt and find happiness, whatever the circumstances? Looking at the world through these new glasses, where I am not concerned only for myself, is disquieting.

I channelled these feelings into *A Mother's Worry*. My two kids perch precariously on the edge of a cliffside with churning waters below them and an ominous sky above them. Unfortunately, this is too often how I feel about the world in which they live. I think that all mothers of every generation have worries for their children and their futures, but the current time period feels like a time when we have even more to worry about: environmental concerns, challenges to social justice and equity, violence, the economy. It's a lot to navigate as a parent, and I think mothers in particular have a unique way of internalizing worry, maybe because we are so used to carrying the weight of so many things at one time. Mothers go from worrying about whether their children are speaking on time, growing at the right rate, or eating well enough, straight to whether there will be a planet for them to live on in 50 years. I wonder what my own mother thought of the frights of her age, such as apocalyptic nuclear warfare, and why she never said anything. Silent worry just seems to be part of the motherhood job description.

A Mother's Worry, 20.5" x 30", wool and acrylic yarns on rug warp. Karen D. Miller, Ottawa, Ontario, Canada, 2018.

Mothers in many parts of the world have to navigate additional and more immediate concerns for their children, such as finding clean water and food for their families, war and violence, disease and access to adequate health care. How do these worries and challenges affect mothers and their children? Linda Friedman Schmidt's piece *When Mothers Can't Mother* is her outcry for peace in the face of rising tension, discrimination, divisiveness, violence, and global unrest. Linda's own experience being raised by a mother traumatized by war has made her acutely aware that children require their mother's love, affection, and availability for their well-being and healthy development.

As Linda tells it, mothers who are "traumatized, downtrodden, or discarded by society" have a hard time connecting with their children, become disengaged, and are unaware that they are unable to care for their children. She strongly believes that the "nurturing response" of a mother to her child is a "model for human interaction," and so when a mother is unable to mother her children, that model disappears, which in turn leads to multiple problems for generations to come. Linda points out that mothers who are "terrorized, grieving, hungry, preoccupied, distressed, and depressed" become incapable of providing their children with emotional support and are unable to recognize that their own trauma becomes transferred to their children. It is this "intergenerational transfer of trauma," such as she herself suffered, that pains Linda to see repeated because "an endangered world affects mothering, which in turn affects the world's future."

> When there is no nurture, what is the future? A generation of innocents will become lasting casualties of negative childhood experiences.
>
> Linda Friedman Schmidt

When Mothers Can't Mother, 63" x 41", discarded clothing. Linda Friedman Schmidt, New York Metro Area, USA, 2003.

At the time that I started to write this book, the world was overtaken by a global pandemic. It is hard to overstate the impact that COVID-19 has had, particularly on mothers. With the shutdown of schools and childcare, mothers have left the workforce at a higher rate than others in order to care for their children. Those mothers who have stayed in their jobs have also had to adapt. Essential workers have had the added stress of having to leave their homes to work and possibly be exposed to the virus. At the same time, childcare options are limited. For those who are able to move their work to their homes, many have had to balance their own work with helping their children with online schooling. This often means balancing kids on their laps during work Zoom calls or putting in an extra shift of work in the evenings once their kids are in bed. Several studies have indicated that mothers during the pandemic have taken on the equivalent of two full-time jobs. This increased balancing act that mothers are required to do, and the move to remote work in the home, is having the effect of magnifying preexisting stereotypes that mothers are caregivers first and foremost and are not as committed to the workplace as their male counterparts.

Mothers also face pressure to keep their children amused, filling the gaps left behind by the disappearance of playdates, birthday parties, and extracurricular activities. Health and safety protocols mean more cleaning and more worry. How can I keep my children safe? What are the long-term impacts for children if they do get the virus? And there is always judgment from others. In the early days of the virus, many single mothers were judged for taking their children with them to the grocery store, which was seen as increasing their risk of getting the virus, even if those women had no alternate childcare available to them.

In my own situation, my kids ended up doing online learning almost 80 percent of the time that I was writing this book. Thankfully, my children are old enough to navigate the technology and class scheduling for the most part on their own, but I still had many more interruptions than I had bargained for when I signed the contract. Although my husband was also working from home, when his door was closed (which was virtually always) the kids knew not to interrupt. I, on the other hand, knew that I couldn't close my door as someone had to be available to help when something couldn't be found, or the laptop was glitching, or they needed a snack. Again, yes, I am well aware that my experience was a comparatively fortunate one and that the experience for visible minorities and those of lesser means was far more fraught.

> . . . it is more specifically mothers who are most impacted by the pandemic because it is mothers who are doing the necessary and arduous carework to sustain our families and communities. However, few are recognizing, let alone supporting, mothers as frontline workers or acknowledging and appreciating what mothers are managing and accomplishing in their homes under unimaginable circumstances.
>
> **Andrea O'Reilly and Fiona Joy Green in** *Mothers, Mothering, and COVID-19: Dispatches from a Pandemic* **[Demeter Press, 2021. Pg. 18]**

On top of all of the extra work and challenges that mothers are facing due to the pandemic, there is also the difficulty of watching your children navigate all of the new protocols, even if you know that it is for their own safety. For the most part, children have adapted much better than many adults, but the first time I saw my own two children wearing masks it really affected me. What is this new world that they are living in? Will I be able to keep them safe? Will their whole childhood be this way? Will things ever be normal again?

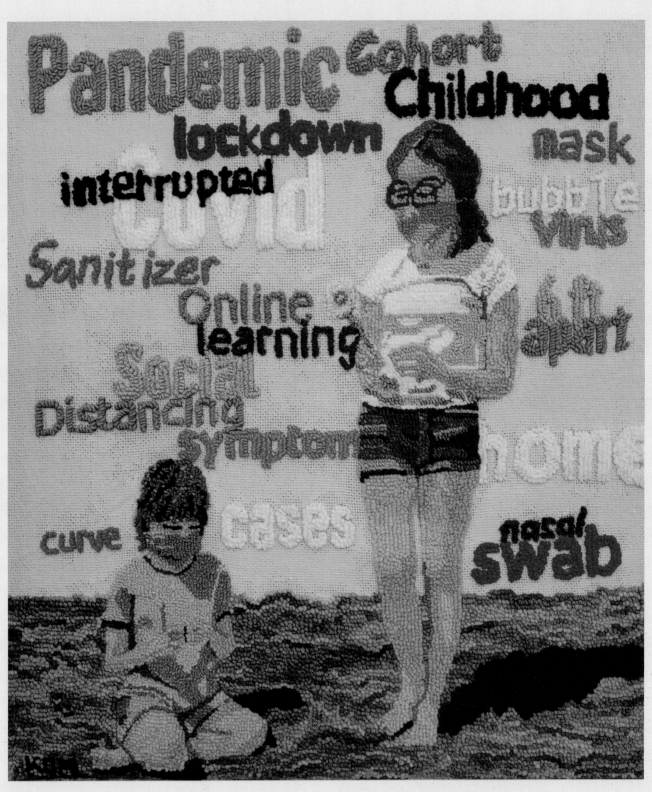

Childhood Interrupted, 22" x 19", wool and acrylic yarns and acrylic paint on rug warp.
Karen D. Miller, Ottawa, Ontario, Canada, 2021.

We have been very fortunate to have stayed healthy, to have a safe home to shelter in and access to all of the amenities that we need. But one area that has brought me a fair amount of stress is making the decision whether to send my children to school or to choose the online education option. Where I live, after the initial shutdown, parents were given the choice for the following school year to either send their children to school or to do remote learning. While being in the fortunate position of having a choice to make, how can you know which is the best choice? There were arguments on both sides of course. If you don't send your children to school, you are depriving them of social interaction and putting their mental health at risk. But if you do send them, you are potentially exposing them to the virus.

At the end of the day, I, like most mothers, just had to make the choice that worked best for my family, and take solace knowing that I had done the best I could with all of the unknowns that I faced. There was no clear-cut right or wrong approach. After much agonizing, I did send my children back to school, armed with their personal bottles of hand sanitizer (the biggest in the class, I am told), extra masks, and strict instructions to wash their hands often. While for the most part I was pleased with the protocols put into place, I was disappointed that lowering class sizes was not one of the measures taken, despite the focus that was being placed on keeping six feet apart in the larger community. I intended *Distancing* to capture the frustrations that I felt about class sizes and the difficult decision that sending my kids to school was for me.

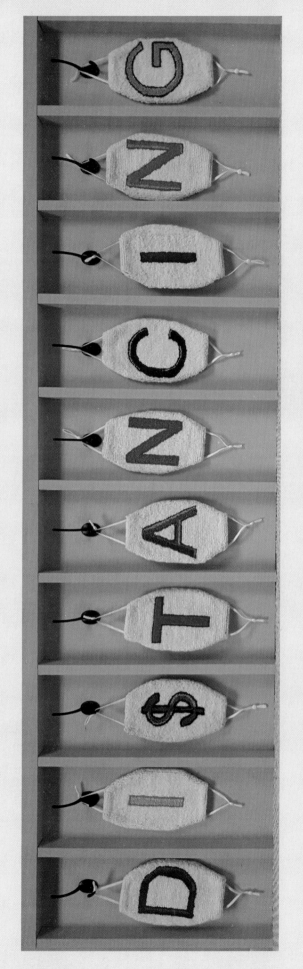

Distancing, 20" x 73", wool and acrylic yarns on linen, coat hooks, and wood. Karen D. Miller, Ottawa, Ontario, Canada, 2021.

Technical Study: The Message in the Medium

In the hands of artists, the fibre we use is often part of the story that we tell. Many of us dye our own textiles and so, just like painters with their paints, we have complete control over every value of every colour that we hook, weave, or stitch. But even more than that, we are also aware that we have more opportunity than many other kinds of artists to invest ourselves into our pieces through our choices of more unusual textiles. Sometimes, these choices are practical, enabling us to achieve different visual effects. And sometimes they are emotional choices, allowing us to emphasize symbolic or deeply personal meanings in our work.

Many of the artists in this book made these kinds of choices. I have a couple of reasons for exploring these choices all together in this separate case study. First, I think it is instructive to examine some of the unusual textile choices made by many of the contributing artists, and why they made them. There are some similarities in the stories that each of these artists told me about why they chose certain materials and why those choices were important to their work and their message.

Second, I want to challenge you to read each of the artists' explanations for their textile choices and look at their finished pieces. I want you to ask yourself if, as the artist intended, the additional knowledge changes what and how you think about the piece. I think that understanding your own reactions to these choices is the surest way for you to understand how you might wish to incorporate similar choices into your own work.

To demonstrate what I mean, I'll start with Meryl Cook's *This Cord of Love that Binds Us* (p. 97). It features a cord symbolic of the connection between her and her youngest son. The symbolism of the cord is quite evident. But what if I told you that the cord in the piece was not clipped from a longer, manufactured cord, just cut to size, and then attached? What if I told you that Meryl, the artist and the mother, made that cord herself, from her own handspun yarn? Does that change your perception of the piece?

I thought so.

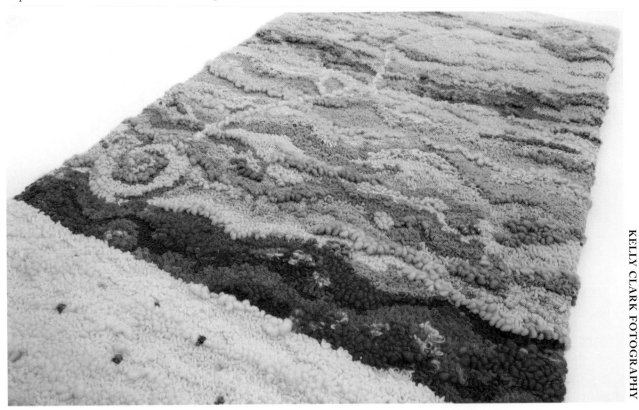

This Cord of Love that Binds Us (detail), 51" x 25.5", wool fabric, yarns, sari cotton, and silk on linen.
Meryl Cook, Dartmouth, Nova Scotia, Canada, 2019.

Several pieces in this book repurpose or recycle previously used materials. There is no question that this can be risky. Fibre art is all too easily dismissed as craft, regardless of the sophistication of the imagery or the skill of the execution. When such viewers perceive the use of repurposed materials, it can sometimes just reinforce their bias that such work is not "art." I wanted to show you several of the examples in this book where repurposing materials was a deliberate and and successful step in the artistic process.

Laura Salamy was feeling something about motherhood that many mothers will sympathize with; she was feeling "worn away." She also observed, as we all have, that the other thing being worn away at the same time was her daughter's clothing. Starting at the knees and the elbows, I would imagine, but I am only speculating. So, when she made *Holes* (p. 27), it was natural that she would use strips of recycled children's clothing and baby textiles, directly conveying her concept that "motherhood, while enriching, can also leave you in tatters." Similarly, Emily van Lidth de Jeude wanted to convey her feelings about the expectations placed on her as a woman that she should strive to marry and have children. By creating her piece *Maternity Wear* (p. 53) on an upcycled wedding dress, she confronts the viewer with something unexpected. And unexpected is exactly what she wants to say to the viewer about how those two life goals can turn out.

GARY LAMOTT

Holes (detail), 68" x 33" x 0.75", recycled textiles, silk sari yarn, and cotton binding on monk's cloth.
Laura Salamy, Albuquerque, New Mexico, USA, 2020.

Linda Friedman Schmidt uses discarded clothing and blankets to create the loops in her pieces *When Mothers Can't Mother* (p. 73) and *Mother Me* (p. 69). For Linda, these textiles reference "comfort, protection, warmth, and nurturing" akin to the attributes that we ascribe to mothers. She is making a strong statement by using them in pieces where she evokes "the pain of a child longing for love."

Amy Meissner uses textile work created by women in the past and in the present to imbue her pieces with further meaning. When Amy was given a number of crocheted doilies, she removed the flowers and used them in her piece, *Descent* (p. 45). At first, she was dismissive of these textiles in "colours representing another era and aesthetic, some other woman's ideal," and wondered if they represented nothing more than some other woman's waste of time and now her own. However, when she massed the flowers together, she realized that they became "achingly beautiful" to look at. When combined with the black form in the centre of the piece representing her journey with postpartum depression, she believes that the piece presents "an opportunity to connect with people on a tactile level, to perhaps pull them into a conversation about something meaningful without being overt and confrontational."

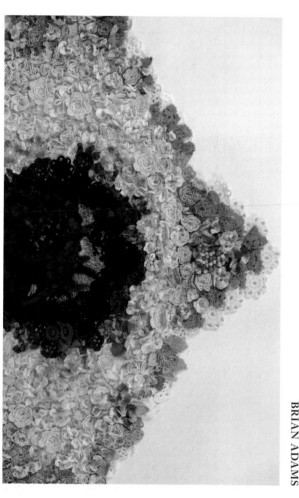

BRIAN ADAMS

Descent (detail), 35" x 53" (suspended component 20" x 9" x 9"), vintage doilies, silk organza, rubber, wire, epoxy clay, and light. Amy Meissner, Anchorage, Alaska, USA, 2017.

I am conceptually rescuing discarded, disposable humanity, cutting up the pain and suffering transferred to me. I transform that which was unconsciously transmitted to me, the sadness, pain, guilt which is represented by the old clothes. Metaphorically, rugs represent the downtrodden I take off the floor. Topics usually swept under the rug are depicted on the surface to encourage discussion of issues otherwise avoided. The weight of the hooked work matches the weight and gravity of the trauma my mother transferred to me and that has weighed on my shoulders.

Linda Friedman Schmidt

In *Shadow Self* (p. 28), Amy uses wool letters to create a repetition of the words "mother" and "other." The words are hand-appliquéd to the reverse sides of abandoned and unfinished embroideries that were donated to her. The women who began these projects are for the most part anonymous, their incomplete handwork unlabelled and unsigned. By building on their work, though, Amy imbues them with new meaning for the next generation of women and mothers.

Linda Rae Coughlin and Michelle Kingdom both chose to stage their work on garments that held meaning for them. Linda Rae often uses upcycled materials in her work, but the antique baby jacket that she uses in her piece *Couldn't* (p. 7) has a particular story. The jacket was from a friend who had dressed her own child in it and then saved it for over 60 years. When she presented it to Linda Rae, Linda Rae could see the joy on her friend's face as she remembered being a mother so long ago. By using the jacket in her art piece, Linda Rae feels that it has a function again and lives on. *For The Propagation of Daughters* (p. 35), Michelle uses a vintage, tattered handkerchief in order to convey the "fragility and vulnerability" of motherhood. The handkerchief was a family textile, purposefully selected for its imperfections to echo the "weathering of living." Michelle found that stitching on a damaged piece was difficult, but that those challenges made it even more appropriate to the piece and "enhanced its meaning and symbolism."

BRIAN ADAMS

Shadow Self (detail), 66" x 66", abandoned embroideries, cotton, velvet, and linen.
Amy Meissner, Anchorage, Alaska, USA, 2019.

Amy Meissner created *Spontaneous Combustion* (p. 57), on what she refers to as "layers of domesticity"—embroidered tea towels, linens, doilies, and curtains—that were created at a time and by a culture that saw them as too "precious" to use. But she also included textiles from those closest to her, such as her husband's cut-up shirts, her children's clothing, and her wedding handkerchief. Doing so allowed her to stitch "upon my own fear of losing these things, these people." Before completing the piece, she had her children make marks and drawings around the border to make the work feel less "precious and beautiful." Her children's mark-making created a further layer to the narrative of the piece, and for Amy "the act of following my children's lines gave me greater insight as to who they were at that moment, and that that time is absolutely gone forever."

BRIAN ADAMS

Spontaneous Combustion (detail), 77" x 54", wool, cotton, and vintage domestic linens; machine pieced, hand embroidered, hand appliquéd, and hand quilted. Amy Meissner, Anchorage, Alaska, USA, 2013.

And to conclude this study, Carmen Bohn incorporated inherited yarns, the first yarns that she had ever hand spun years before, and even a favourite t-shirt that she used to love, into *This Is the Unfinished Story of So Many Things No. 2* (p. 13). As such, her weaving became a place for "a lot of the stories that finally get to look out from the wall of my studio rather than be piled up in plastic bags at the bottom of a storage space." If you look really closely, you will also see a tiny mirror that she has included. Carmen says it was once her daughter's and "mysteriously" ended up in her stash, like it was "begging to reflect back some new adventures in this new life."

This Is the Unfinished Story of So Many Things No. 2 (detail), 38" x 33", hand-spun yarns, fabric, yarn, recycled sari silk, t-shirt, and mirror. Carmen Bohn, Ottawa, Ontario, Canada, 2021.

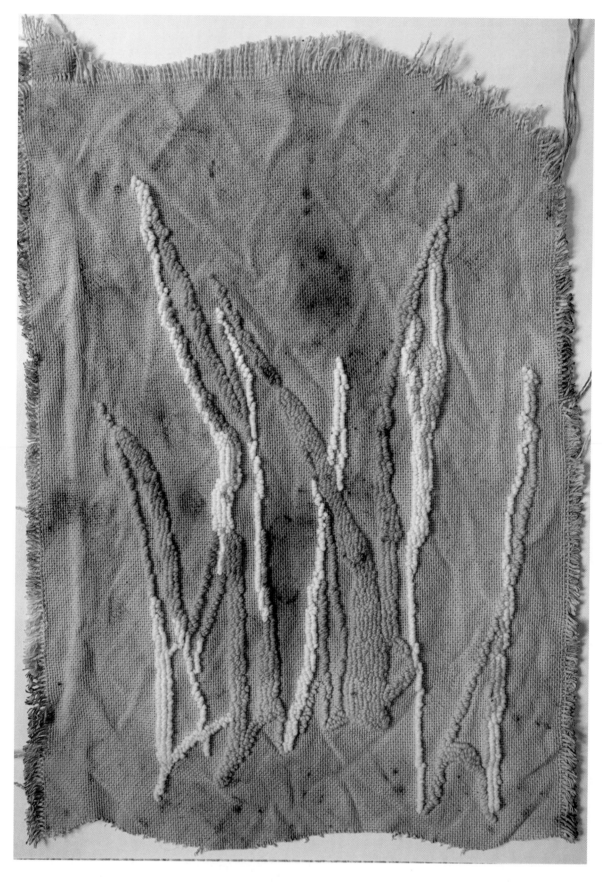

Marks of Motherhood XIII, 22.5" x 16.5" rust-dyed wool yarn on rug warp. Karen D. Miller, Ottawa, Ontario, Canada, 2021.

7

Endings

When your baby first comes into your life, the whole idea that you could ever be in control is laughable. You feed, you clean up—hopefully you even sleep. Somewhere out there, a world goes by and largely, you don't notice. Salvation comes with routine. Teaching baby about the existence of night and sleep between feedings is an enormous victory. It is the death of spontaneity, but a price well worth paying. For a time, life has a bearable balance. But then it changes again, when the new being in your family ceases just being alive and responsive and becomes meaningfully sentient. You notice that there is something else in their gaze when they look back at you—less stimulus-response and more recognizably thoughtful. Slowly, they begin asserting themselves in the world. They test and experiment, and since you are still most of their world, that means experimenting on you, mostly by screaming "no!" and hurling food on the floor. Thus, ingloriously, begins their long road to independence and the preordained end of your pole position in their life. And yet, part of why we love so unconditionally is because of what we put in of ourselves.

Motherhood is like no other relationship in our lives; it is far more personal than our causes, our careers, even our marriages. We took for granted our own mother's sacrifices, and we invest ourselves just as wholly in our own children as our own mothers did in us.

Everyone negotiates this journey with their child in their own way, but fundamentally every parent is travelling the same journey of gradually ceding choice and responsibility until nothing is left. We all have our own perspectives on how much control we exercise over this journey. My husband seemed to concede this question very early with regards to our first child when he decided that they were like a rocket. "They've launched," he said, "and they're going wherever they're going."

The woman with a large, circular hole in the middle of her abdomen in *Little by Little, There was Scarcely Anything Left* (p. 86), by Michelle Kingdom, is a mother who is "weary" and has "given her all, now worn at the very center." Behind the mother is her child, who represents all of the mother's "hopes and dreams, which she gladly makes way for." In Michelle's view, all children face struggles as they grow, and watching our children navigate through the "hard parts of life" is one of the "hardest things to live through as a parent." She explains that "the fantasy of motherhood merely skims the surface," and in reality, all mothers must "walk through fire" in order to "really understand the helplessness and desperation one feels watching your own child's hardships and not being able to save them."

Love Many, Trust Few (p. 87) is based on a photo of Trish Johnson's son when he was 15 and headed off to summer camp. Trish, like most mothers, worried about him being "cold, or wet, or hungry" while he was away. But she knew that she had to metaphorically and literally allow him to "paddle his own canoe" and trust that he would make it through this new and challenging experience. Trish explains that her piece is about encouraging our kids to be themselves and giving them advice to guide them, but at the same time understanding that they may choose to ignore our advice and that is part of the growing process, too.

> **There are so many examples of when it's appropriate to be the eyes-shut mother . . . if they choose a path that leads to mistakes, perhaps even mistakes we could have foreseen, we need to let them make and own those errors and learn from them.**
>
> **Elizabeth Miller**

Little by Little, There was Scarcely Anything Left, 4" x 3", hand embroidery on silk.
Michelle Kingdom, Burbank, California, USA, 2014.

Love Many, Trust Few, 13.3" x 13.3", wool on linen. Trish Johnson, Toronto, Ontario, Canada, 2003.

Success as a mother means that you have children who can survive on their own.

Trish Johnson

As mothers, we need to fully see our children as who they are, not as reflections of who we are, who we wanted to be, or who we thought we wanted them to be.

Elizabeth Miller

Like Trish, and like all mothers, I have had many of those moments as well. My piece *The Tree Climber* captures what was probably one of the first times I realized that I would have to stand back as a mother and let my children grow and discover on their own. The piece was inspired by a moment with my eldest child at the park when they were three years old. My husband had helped with climbing the lower branches of the tree and then had let go. My child looked so proud, balancing there all alone. There was no risk—it wasn't high—but I remember catching my breath. It was a moment of independence that to that point hadn't happened much given their young age. I realized then that this was my future, watching many more of these moments that would only grow in frequency and scale. I was right, there have been many such moments with both children, and each time they happen I try to remember to stand back, take a breath, let them find their own footing, and just be an observer as they write their own life stories.

Footloose and Fancy Free (p. 90) is not just a memory captured of April DeConick's son and his two cousins at the Galveston pier one Christmas. This piece has also helped her to face the "bittersweet" parts of motherhood, where we carry out our responsibility to guide our children into adulthood, all the while knowing that "the cherished moments of childhood freedom will soon be but memories." When she took the photo, none of them knew that it would be the "last gasp of childhood" when the three would play together as children. April says that so many memories are like that, because as a mother you never quite know when it will be the last time for something: the last time they take your hand to cross the road, or the last bedtime story. Now that her son is older, April feels "less and less certain" how to guide him because he is now at an age when he doesn't necessarily want guidance. Yet at the same time, she feels that it may be the time when he could use guidance the most. She feels hopeful, though, that she was able to guide him enough when he was younger that he will make "good choices" as he grows.

My children are still fairly young, but I am not immune to thoughts of their growing up and needing me less. I love to take photos of our shadows every now and again: on the pavement, on the grass, on the snow in winter. Sometimes it is just myself and my son from when I drop him off to school in the mornings and we are the first ones on the school yard. Sometimes they are of myself and both of my kids when we are out on a walk at the right time of day. When I look back at these shadow photos that I have taken over the years, I am struck by how they still show so much change even with such little detail. Even though they are often distorted by the sun and our shadows often take on gigantic proportions, I can still track my children's growth as they race towards my own height. Just as the placement of the sun changes our shadows, so too does time change our relationship. My trio of small pieces, *In the Shadows* (p. 91), is about the mixed feelings that I have about watching them grow and become more and more independent.

> From our bodies come new life, life that is not ours to hold or keep, but to nurture and set free. In motherhood, loss and relinquishment are the catalysts for new life.
>
> **April DeConick**

> One of the hardest parts of being a mother is letting your children go.
>
> **Trish Johnson**

The Tree Climber, 15" x 18.5", wool, acrylic and metallic yarns on linen. Karen D. Miller, Ottawa, Ontario, Canada, 2011.

Footloose and Fancy Free, 18" x 33", wool on linen. April DeConick, Houston, Texas, USA, 2018.

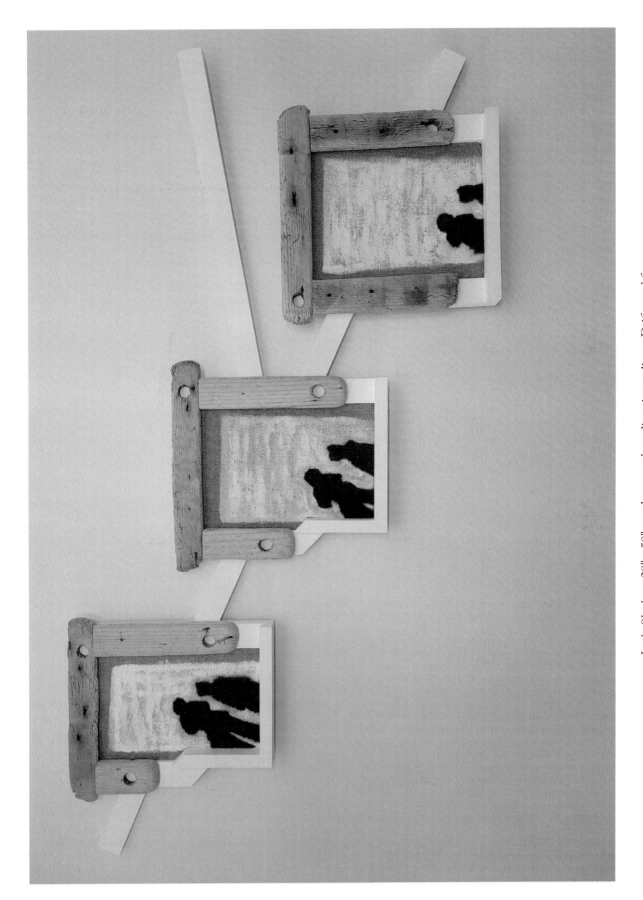

In the Shadows, 29" x 50", wool yarn and acrylic paint on linen. Driftwood frame.
Karen D. Miller, Ottawa, Ontario, Canada, 2021. Driftwood frame by Daniel MacDonald.

Chris and Blackie: Summer of 1977 began as a photograph of Trish Johnson's mother that was taken the summer before her mother's cancer diagnosis. The text in the piece came from one of a number of letters that her mother typed to her. Trish and her sister were both living in Toronto at the time, and her mother was left behind in Capreol, a small isolated town in Northern Ontario, with Trish's father who, as her mother writes, "let the TV do the talking for him." Trish's sister and her baby had lived in Capreol up until a month before this letter was written, and so her mother was dealing with a new sense of loneliness and adjusting to a new normal.

Trish reads this letter differently now than she did when she first received it all those years ago, and says "now I know what she means." At the time that Trish was making her piece, she had only her youngest child still living at home, and so while she didn't quite have an empty nest, she could "see it coming" and "realized that my life was going to be like my mother's." Just as we all eventually have to deal with our children growing up and going off into the world on their own, Trish could see that soon "it was just going to be me and my husband. It had come full cycle, back to how it was at the beginning."

It is no accident that Ellen Skea Marshall's piece *Foundation to Flight* (p. 94) includes the foundation of a house and three birds in flight in the sky above. She explains that they represent the importance she placed on providing a solid footing for her three children while also allowing them to grow and become independent. Ellen didn't always find it easy to let go, and when her eldest daughter left home to go to college, she felt like a piece of her was missing. Once she adapted to this change in her life, though, it became somewhat easier for her when the time came for each of her other two children to leave and go off into the world.

The paths that her children took weren't always straight—"there were definitely bumps along the way"—and Ellen represents this with the winding path through her piece. But in the end, each of her children found their way and Ellen is extremely proud of all of their accomplishments. It makes her happy that her children "know that they will always be able to depend on my husband and I for support," but that they also understand that "we have given them the basics to be good adults."

Sometimes, though, letting go of our children can be a bit more complicated. *Rejection* (p. 95) is a case in point, as Laura Salamy represents her relationship with her daughter that she describes as "irregular." It isn't the close mother-daughter relationship that Laura was perhaps expecting and, as a result, letting go has instead been more of what she describes as a "controlled pushing away" to show her daughter that she can be her own person and make her own decisions, and to give her the opportunity to be a "self-sufficient adult."

Laura has found balancing the compulsion to check on her daughter to make "sure she is doing what she needs to be doing"—with the resulting exhaustion and stress—challenging, and says that "it's difficult to determine when to intervene as a child gets older," particularly when that child "has had issues throughout childhood." She feels sadness that because of the challenges that her daughter experiences, their relationship has remained one of mother-child even into adulthood, rather than evolving into more of a friendship. Yet true to the concept of the duality of motherhood, Laura still wishes that her daughter lived closer to her, despite all of the struggles in their relationship.

> **Holding on to her can be like holding on to clouds, usually storm clouds. But I do occasionally see some blue sky.**
>
> **Laura Salamy**

Chris and Blackie: Summer of 1977, 24" x 36.5", wool on linen. Trish Johnson, Toronto, Ontario, Canada, 2006.

Foundation to Flight, 31" x 14.5", wool, hand-dyed wool, and yarns on linen. Ellen Skea Marshall, Bethel, Maine, USA, 2021.

Rejection, 14" x 17.5", wool strips and yarn on monk's cloth. Laura Salamy, Albuquerque, New Mexico, USA, 2021.

However badly we want to have all of the answers that our children assume of us, we know that it isn't the case. Like everything else in life, parenting is complicated, self-contradictory, inconsistent, and messy. Our job is to protect and shelter, but sometimes we just can't. Sometimes the fates intervene and they simply bear all before them in storms that can only be ridden out as best as one can. When children are younger, sometimes this can take the form of illness. Ellen Skea Marshall's middle daughter became very ill when she was five years old, and Ellen spent much time with her in the ICU, caring for her. It was a very frightening time for Ellen, one in which she had very little control over the situation, so she threw all of her time and attention into doing what she could to help her daughter pull through and eventually recover. Similarly, Jane Smith's eldest son was born ten weeks premature and spent the first six weeks of his life in intensive care. Jane visited him daily and remembers that it was a "very dark time" until he started to get better.

And sometimes we lose control when our children are older and they make choices that we may not agree with. Meryl Cook's piece *This Cord of Love that Binds Us* was created during a very stressful time for her when her son was facing incarceration. She found herself struggling with how to be his mother and provide him with support, but at the same time to not be responsible for his emotional well-being as an adult child and to not be constantly pulled into his challenges, thereby putting her own life on hold. This was not an easy thing to navigate, and Meryl acknowledges that no matter whether you birthed your child or they came to you some other way, all parents have "an energetic cord of love connecting us to them."

Working on this piece allowed Meryl to come to terms with the fact that each of her sons was doing what he needed to be doing and that she did not need to worry or carry it for them. Most importantly, she came to realize that "the best, most loving thing that I can do for each of them is to take care of myself and be the person I was always meant to be." Key to Meryl making this realization was recognizing that unconditional love changes as our children grow. She explains that when our children are young, it is fairly easy for us as mothers to love them unconditionally as there is not much that they can do that we would find "unforgivable." However, as our children grow, they sometimes make "choices that go against what we believe." At that stage, we need to learn to give unconditional love without having any sort of expectations attached to it, as then we won't "take it personally if their choices put them in conflict with our core beliefs." When Meryl recognized that "it's not their job to live to please us, it's their job to live their lives," her own healing was able to begin.

This love

Connecting Us

Thread

A Filament that is thin at times,

But strong and resilient like silk.

No matter where you are or where life takes each of us,

We will remain connected by this thread of love

It has been there since your beginning, in my womb

And maybe since our previous lives.

You may feel very far away, but this translucent, strong thread will remain.

Keeping our love fastened to one another, telling us both—you are loved.

This thread of love, connecting us, a bond of love.

— Meryl Cook

This Cord of Love that Binds Us, 51" x 25.5", wool fabric, yarns, sari cotton, and silk on linen.
Meryl Cook, Dartmouth, Nova Scotia, Canada, 2019.

And unfortunately, we must acknowledge that the worst part of life is the end, and that it may come to pass that as a mother we will not be able to protect our children from death. In fact, it is far more common for a mother to lose a child than you might think, because to a large degree we still choose to be blind to it.

A number of the artists contributing to this book were very open about their experience with miscarriage, describing it as "without doubt the most acutely painful event in my life" that left them feeling "completely empty both emotionally and physically." Universally, the women mentioned that even today, loss of a child through miscarriage is something that is not really talked about or acknowledged. One artist said that when it happened to her, there was barely any discussion about it "beyond the clinical" with her doctor, and while she felt some support from other women who were close to her, for the most part, "in the wider world a woman suffering this kind of loss was expected to pull her body back together and emotionally move on."

A loss that nobody can fail to acknowledge is that of an adult child, but even then it can be misunderstood. When Jane Smith lost her adult son, she tried hard to keep herself together for her other son and her husband. She kept up her routines and tried to stay engaged in life around her so that she could be there for them, knowing that if she crumbled, they all would. Jane says that by choosing to stay strong for her family, she faced a lot of judgment and felt that people around her were telling her how to grieve. She observes that "people do not know how to react sometimes" and that many were very clear that "they feel that there is a certain way to behave" when you are experiencing loss. What those around her didn't understand, though, was that Jane was grieving during those moments when she felt that she could let her guard down.

One of Jane's biggest worries was that of losing her son's memory or having it fade over time. She wanted to keep him close to her, "if not in life then in spirit." Keeping this connection was extremely important, and she says "I can manage the new normal of having him no longer with us as long as I still have a connection with him." For Jane, creating her piece *William* was a new way of connecting herself to him. Working on the piece brought up happy memories and was a way for Jane to honour him. The photo on which the piece was based is one of her favourites because she "caught the moment when my son's emotional guard was down . . . a more vulnerable photo." To other mothers who may be grieving the loss of a child, Jane says that "while you may never experience absolute joy anymore, you can, if possible, keep your child's memory alive in any way that feels natural and comfortable with you."

> In watching my four sons grow into four very different, but very connected, individuals, I sometimes wonder what kind of people the four who didn't make it would have been.
>
> **Elizabeth Miller**

William, 11" x 12", yarns on linen. Jane Smith, Ottawa, Ontario, Canada, 2019.

8

What Next?

In a society that equates womanhood with motherhood, what happens when the day-to-day hands-on mothering ends? Where does that leave women? What are the supports for women to get back into the workplace if they took a break, and how do employers value the time that they took to mother? How do judgments and assumptions affect mothers who now want this to be their time, after having given so much?

What is next for me and who will I become as my children continue to grow and eventually won't need me as much?

I don't know the answers to any of these questions, but everybody discovers their own answers in their own way. The only thing for certain is that one way or the other, I'm going to find out . . . .

> I loved being a stay-at-home mom despite all of the challenges. I put my life on hold so I could give them a good foundation to leap from. Now I am doing something that feels satisfying, yet sometimes indulgent—but that is okay.
>
> **Ellen Skea Marshall**

> I am finally giving myself licence to do more of the things that light me up, every day. I'd like to share the magic and wonder that I am finding in this phase of life, as I reclaim time and own my passion as an artist and entrepreneur.
>
> **Carmen Bohn**

> There are more challenges now as the mother of adult children. I now have a "self" and a life of my own. I need lots of time alone now, more time to take care of myself physically, spiritually, and emotionally.
>
> **Linda Friedman Schmidt**

> I will never be the person I was before I became a mother, and I will never have absolute freedom, but that is okay.
>
> **Sayward Johnson**

Evolving Identity, 17" x 13.5", wool and acrylic yarns on rug warp. Karen D. Miller, Ottawa, Ontario, Canada, 2021.

Other Contributing Artists

Alexandrya Eaton is a contemporary Canadian painter whose studio practice has grown to include rug hooking and weaving. Using a vibrant palette and simplified shapes, she explores phases of womanhood in her contemporary imagery. Alexandrya lives and works in Sackville, New Brunswick, Canada. www.alexandryaeaton.com

Amy Meissner combines traditional handwork, found objects, and abandoned textiles to reference the literal, physical, and emotional labour of women. Her work is traditional, fine and craft-based, relying on the repetitive nature of hand stitching to relay a manic and confrontational feminist subject matter. Her intent is to create thoughtful, arresting work, reliant on layers of narrative within the pieces themselves and within the history each viewer brings. Amy has an undergraduate degree in art and textiles, an MFA in creative writing and an MA in critical craft studies. She lives and works in Anchorage, Alaska, USA. www.amymeissner.com

April DeConick is captivated by the power of colour to arouse emotion and meaning, and to uplift and inspire. She explores the transcendence of colour and texture through abstraction and collages translated to hooked wool surfaces. Through her work, she invites the audience to reach out and touch colour. April lives and works in Houston, Texas, USA. www.aprildeconick.art

Carmen Bohn is a modern fibre artist, creative entrepreneur, and educator. She reclaims and upcycles textiles and household waste to create her own spun yarns, woven tapestries, and free-form crocheted and knitted pieces. Creating fibre art with a textural and colourful message is her heart's passion. Carmen lives and works in Ottawa, Ontario, Canada. www.plystudio613.com

Elizabeth Miller is an avid homesteader, and themes from her gardens, bee keeping, and chicken keeping often find their way into her designs. She is also inspired by the beauty of her natural surroundings in Maine. Elizabeth feels that it is particularly important to perpetuate artisanship into the next century and she promotes these skills regularly through teaching and public outreach. Elizabeth lives and works in Paris, Maine, USA. www.parrishousewoolworks.com

Ellen Skea Marshall grew up walking on her grandmother's hooked rugs, and from her first pulled loop she knew it was an art form that spoke to her. Ellen adheres to the traditions of this craft but gives her work a modern twist through her choice of design elements and materials. Ellen lives and works in Bethel, Maine, USA. www.twocatsanddoghooking.com

Emily van Lidth de Jeude is a social practice artist, working through art and education to promote social and environmental engagement and to open communication about issues of human evolution. Much of her work is interview-based, and many of the materials she uses are reclaimed, having a history of use by women, children, and families. Emily lives and works on Bowen Island/Nexwlélexm, British Columbia, Canada. www.emilyartist.ca

Jane Smith's hooked rugs create tangible reminders of her favourite moments and memories. She is inspired by her sons and the natural surroundings at her cottage in Newfoundland & Labrador, Canada. Her work has recently been chosen as a finalist for *Rug Hooking* Magazine's *Celebration of Hand Hooked Rugs 32*. Jane lives and works in Ottawa, Ontario, Canada. @blogginthebay

Karen Larsen combines her love of rug hooking with her extensive experience in graphic design to create images that relay her messages in simple yet bold ways. Karen lives and works in Elliottsburg, Pennsylvania, USA

Laura Salamy creates "not so traditional" textile pieces with an emphasis on using reclaimed materials. As an inhabitant of an earth on the cusp of environmental disaster, and with a background in environmental science and regulation, reusing materials rather than discarding them is an essential part of Laura's art practice. Laura lives and works in Albuquerque, New Mexico, USA. www.highonhooking.com.

Linda Friedman Schmidt's emotional narrative portraits encapsulate memories and feelings that overlap with the collective female experience. Linda transforms and breathes new life into discarded clothing embedded with identity and haunting history. She portrays the self and others in pieces, multilayered fragments of hand-cut clothing; she deconstructs and reconstructs layers of the past to create something new. Her artwork inspires empathy and furthers our understanding of the human condition. She brings the craft of rug hooking into a global contemporary art context. Linda lives and works in the New York metropolitan area, USA. www.lindafriedmanschmidt.com

Linda Rae Coughlin creates hooked and stitched textile art to capture her intuitive guidance and follow it where it may lead, even when society may not feel comfortable with some of the issues she raises. Her current work is rooted in feminism and looks at women and the issues and events that challenge their lives. Linda Rae lives and works in Warren, New Jersey, USA. www.theartrugs.com

Lori Laberge is fascinated by the interaction between architecture and geometry, and uses her work to blend line and shape to artistically form new worlds. She uses a variety of materials in a single work to create a combination of stark opposites: soft textile juxtaposed with hard construction materials and oftentimes paint. Lori lives and works in Spruce Pine, North Carolina, USA. www.lorilaberge.com

Meryl Cook's work combines journaling and design to explore fibre art as a process for reinvention and transformation. She selects colours based on Chakra colour theory and a technique of following the healing energy to produce an intuitive, abstract design. Colour, texture, joy, and self-compassion are the key features of Meryl's art. Meryl lives and works in Dartmouth, Nova Scotia, Canada. www.merylcook.ca

Michelle Kingdom's work explores psychological landscapes, illuminating thoughts left unspoken. She creates tiny worlds in thread to capture elusive yet persistent inner voices. While her work acknowledges the luster and lineage inherent in needlework, she uses thread as a sketching tool in order to simultaneously honor and undermine this tradition. Michelle lives and works in Burbank, California, USA. www.michellekingdom.com

Michele Micarelli's work always tells a story, and she uses vibrant colours and attention to detail to add meaning to every piece. After growing up with hooked rugs on the floor that her father had made, she became trained in traditional rug hooking. She creates contemporary designs by combining tradition with the exploration of alternative materials. Michele is a teacher devoted to promoting creativity. She lives and works in New Haven, Connecticut, USA. www.michelemicarelli.com

Nadine Flagel's mission is making art out of "making do," and she believes the most impressive creative traditions come from finding uses for discarded or scrap materials. She enjoys the vibrant juxtapositions of texture and colour that are only possible with reclaimed fabrics. As a trained academic in literature, Nadine finds that rug making is a pursuit worthy of critical thinking and she is intrigued by the intersections between text and textile. Nadine lives and works in Vancouver, British Columbia, Canada. www.pretextstudio.com

Patti Colen marries her love of documentary photography with the technique of rug hooking to create pieces that respond to the world around her. She finds inspiration in political issues, the environment, and the human condition. Patti lives and works in London, Ontario, Canada. @thewoollycrone

Rachelle Leblanc's work is intimate; it provides a tender glimpse into the emotional response to culture and sense of place. The pieces she creates utilizing traditional tools and techniques, when juxtaposed with her contemporary eye, bring an immediacy, an almost urgency, showing emotional depth and beauty using ordinary materials like steel, clay, and fibre, Rachelle lives and works in Katy, Texas, USA. www.rachelleleblanc.com

Sayward Johnson's textile-based works are made with hand-woven copper wire which she then oxidizes with green patina, manipulates, and embroiders. Through her work, she is able to explore her fascination with fabrics that adhere to the laws of metalsmithing as well as those of textiles, and present traditional textile patterns in unexpected contexts. Sayward lives and works in Chelsea, Quebec, Canada. www.saywardjohnson.com

Trish Johnson finds inspiration in the concept of "home" and what it means to her. For her, hooked rugs are not just art but are also visual diaries which capture her childhood memories, family history, and favourite places. Trish lives and works in Toronto, Ontario, Canada. www.trishjohnson.ca

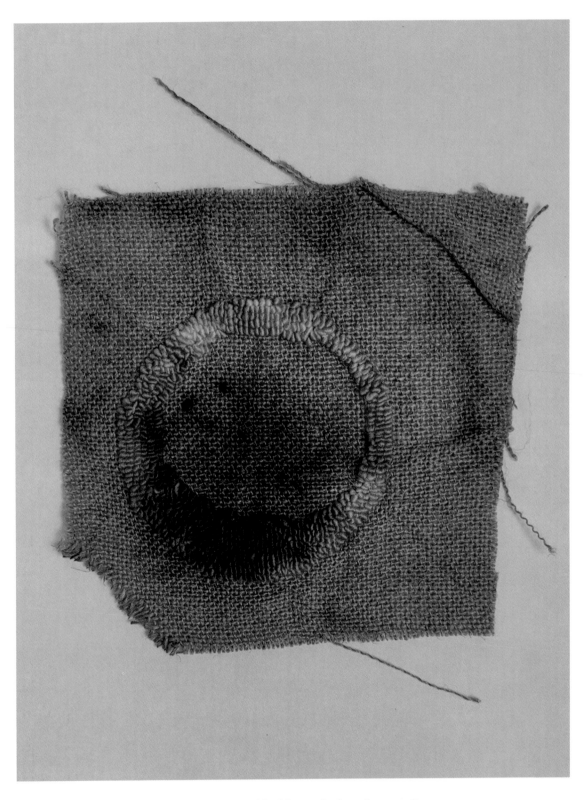

Marks of Motherhood I, 7" x 7", rust-dyed wool yarn on linen.
Karen D. Miller, Ottawa, Ontario, Canada, 2021.

187 School Lunches, 35" x 27.5", wool and acrylic yarns on rug warp.
Karen D. Miller, Ottawa, Ontario, Canada, 2022.